U0538840

戰火・Peace Beyond the Frontlines・和平

抗戰時期美軍眼中的中國
American Soldiers' View of China During WWII

主編 / 楊善堯
翻譯 / 楊宗翰
審閱 / 陳榮彬

作者 / William Tang（唐銘遠）、Ethan Cheung（張健宣）、Aiden Zhang（章容添）

喆閎人文

目次
Contents

06　　Editor's Words 主編序

10　　Introduction
16　　引言

21　　Wartime Refugees
30　　戰時難民

49　　Women and Children
54　　戰時婦孺

67　　Peasants and Kunming
72　　農民與昆明

82　　The Wartime Experience of Peasants
91　　農民的戰時經歷

111　　People
117　　人民

144　　City
151　　城市

171　　Conclusion
175　　結語

179　　References 參考資料

主編序
Editor's Words

This book is a photography album that combines military history, archival images, historical humanities teaching, and international relations between the Republic of China (Taiwan) and the United States.

The origin of this series of historical photo books can be traced back to an international exchange activity. In June 2023, a group of Chinese-American high school students and their parents came to Taiwan under the leadership of Dr. Lin Hsiao-ting(林孝庭), the research fellow from the Hoover Institution of Stanford University. They visited the Presidential Palace, Academia Historica, National Revolutionary Martyrs' Shrine, Chiang Kai-shek Memorial Hall, the Palace Museum, the Grand Hotel, Fu Jen Catholic University, Longshan Temple, Bopiliao Historic Block, Daxi Old Street, and other places with strong "Republican, Chinese, and Taiwanese local culture" style. When they saw these scenic spots, they realized not only the historical and cultural significance behind these sites, but also their connections related to what they learned in the United States and their family backgrounds. This tour gives this group of high school students who came to Taiwan (Republic of China) for the first time a considerable cultural shock. During the visit, they constantly realized that the Republic of China is highly related to the United States where they grew up. This inspired their motivation and interest in exploring this period of history, which was the origin of this book.

Regarding the military cooperation between the Republic of China and the United States in the early twentieth century, it can be traced from the later stages of the War of Resistance against Japanese (1937-1945). When the Chinese government waged a full-scale and arduous warfare, the United States gave China considerable support, from civilian assistance to formal military aids. In the 1950s, while economy of Taiwan gained highly development with the U.S. aids, the military cooperation between the Republic of China and the United States is also a vital part of the Cold War history. The subject of this book, "Wartime Chinese Society from the Perspective of the US Military", is an important part of Sino-American military cooperation.

The three authors of this book, William Tang(唐銘遠)、Ethan Cheung(張健

宣)、Aiden Zhang(章容添), use historical photos and archives collected by the U.S. National Archives, and the Zhe Hong Humanities Studio(喆閎人文工作室) to present the subject clearly and richly through chronological arrangement. The impact of visual images is far greater than the feelings that words bring to readers. I hope the publication of this photo album, interpretation of the historical archives by three high school students, will attract more people's attention to this period of history, and help readers understand that historical archives are not only for scholars, even high school students can use them to complete a project.

Yang, Shan-Yao
2025.5.27

這本書是一本結合軍事歷史、檔案影像、歷史人文教學、中華民國（臺灣）與美國國際關係的攝影冊。

　　這個系列歷史照片書籍的源起，要從一次的國際交流活動談起。2023 年 6 月，一群美籍華裔高中生與家長，在史丹佛大學胡佛研究所林孝庭研究員的帶領下來到了臺灣，在總統府、國史館、忠烈祠、中正紀念堂、故宮博物院、圓山飯店、輔仁大學、龍山寺、剝皮寮、大溪老街等地方進行了參訪與交流，這些帶有濃厚「民國風、中華文化、臺灣在地文化」風格的景點，以及這些景點帶來的實體視覺與景點背後所隱含的歷史文化意義，都與他們從小在美國所學以及家庭文化有所關聯，給了這群第一次來到臺灣（中華民國）的高中生們相當大的文化衝擊。在參訪的過程中，他們不斷地發現到一個問題：「中華民國跟他們所生長的美國有著高度關聯性」，這引起了他們去探索這段歷史過往的動機與興趣，也是這本書誕生的緣起。

　　有關中華民國與美國在二十世紀的軍事往來，可從抗日戰爭的中後期開始談起。在中華民國政府進行全面性的艱苦戰爭時，美國從民間援助到正式軍援，給了當時中華民國政府相當大的支持，到了 1950 年代後，在美援支持下臺灣快速的全面復甦，尤其在軍事上的援助，更是冷戰時代下中華民國與美國的重要連結。這本書所講述的「美軍眼中戰時中國社會」主題，正好是串聯起這段中華民國與美國友好過往的重要歷史。

　　William Tang（唐銘遠）、Ethan Cheung（張健宣）、Aiden Zhang（章容添）三位作者利用美國國家檔案館與喆閎人文工作室所典藏的歷史照片與檔案，透過照片解讀與時序排列，清楚且豐富的呈現出「美軍眼中戰時中國社會」這個主題。視覺影像的渲染力與感受力遠大於單純文字給讀者帶來的感受，希望這本攝影冊的面世，透過作者解讀歷史檔案的過程，能引起更多人對於這段歷史的注意，以及讓歷史人文融入應用實作有更多的成果展現。

楊善堯

民國一一四年五月廿七日

INTRODUCTION

On September 18, 1931, Japan staged a bombing on a railroad in Manchuria, blaming China for the attack as a pretext to invade. This invasion led to the establishment of the puppet state of Manchukuo and sparked the Second Sino-Japanese War. The war initially unfolded through a series of small skirmishes. However, following the Marco Polo Bridge Incident in 1937, the conflict merged with the broader outbreak of World War II, and from 1937 to 1945, the war disrupted millions of lives. Life during these years became a relentless struggle, with many people lacking even basic necessities such as food and clothing. Throughout this period, the American public never lost sight of China's suffering. Support evolved from grassroots efforts to formal government actions, yet the presence of aid and solidarity remained steadfast.

Civilian Assistance

In the early 1930s, the United States military found itself largely unable to provide assistance in the ongoing wars, whether in China or elsewhere. Three primary factors contributed to this limited involvement. First, the country was recovering from the effects of the Great Depression, which had severely strained its economy. With its resources stretched thin, international conflicts were not a priority. Second, the aftermath of the First World War had left many Americans deeply influenced by pacifism and isolationism. Scarred by the horrors of global war, the nation was reluctant to engage in another foreign conflict, particularly one as distant as China's. Finally, the U.S. military was simply too small in comparison to the scale of international needs.

Despite these challenges, private foundations in the United States rallied to support China's war of resistance, driven by a strong sense of solidarity and moral duty. Their contributions, which focused on medical, educational, and social initiatives, became a crucial source of hope during a period when official government aid was limited. With support from many U.S. charitable organizations, orphanages were established to care for refugee children, hospitals were set up to address urgent medical needs, and schools were founded to educate the Chinese people.

In 1940, many of these charities joined together to form a collective organization called the American Federation to Aid China. This organization has made significant contributions, including educating the American public about China's war and assisting Chinese institutions in fundraising. Beyond providing material support, the Federation worked to strengthen the relationship between China and the United States, highlighting the urgent need for American help. Their message was clear and compelling: China was fighting alone against Japanese aggression, and to continue its resistance, it desperately needed the support of the United States.

Economic Support

During WWII, the U.S. provided substantial economic support to China. In 1938, China secured a $25 million "tung oil loan" from the U.S., using tung oil as collateral, with a 4.5% interest rate but restrictions on using the funds for arms. In 1940, China obtained an additional $20 million loan with a 4% interest rate, repayable over seven years. Later, in October 1940, the "Tungsten Sand Loan Contract" provided China with another $25 million, to be repaid with tungsten sand within five years. The "Sino-US Metal Loan Contract" signed in 1941 allowed China to sell minerals worth $60 million to the U.S. in exchange for a $50 million loan, half of which was paid in cash and the rest designated for purchasing industrial and agricultural products from the U.S.

On May 6, 1941, President Roosevelt announced that the Lend-Lease Act would extend to China, stating, "China is vital to the defense of the United States, and China is eligible to receive Lend-Lease assistance." Just over a week later, on May 18, the first shipment of Lend-Lease materials, valued at $1.1 million, including 300 six-wheel trucks, arrived in China from New York. Through the Lend-Lease Act, the United States provided China with substantial military aid, including weapons, aircraft, and ammunition. This support was crucial for China's defense against Japanese aggression and helped maintain some stability for the civilian population. By the end of 1945, American historian Dwight Dumond estimated that the United States had supplied China with $1.335 billion in Lend-Lease aid.

Military Cooperation

After Germany and the Soviet Union invaded Poland in 1939, and Japan joined the Axis powers of Germany and Italy in 1940 before beginning its invasion of Indochina, the United States government came to see the war in China as an American war. The situation became urgent after the Soviet–Japanese Neutrality Pact was signed between Japan and the Soviet Union in 1941 which allowed Japan to redeploy troops from Manchuria and Mongolia to other areas, particularly in Southeast Asia.

In 1941, the United States began providing financial and military support to China through the Lend-Lease Act, which included sending military equipment and training Chinese officers. As part of this, China received 100 P-40 fighter planes, and U.S. Army pilots were permitted to leave their posts to fight in China. This led to the formation of the Flying Tigers, a key symbol of U.S. support that fought in China against the Japanese during the war.

After the attack on Pearl Harbor on December 7, 1941, the United States declared war on Japan, forming an official alliance with China. This led to the creation of the China-Burma-India Theater (CBI), one of the most formidable fronts of World War II. By that time, Japan had already deployed over 800,000 troops in China, supported by a very modern air force and ground military. The situation within China was further complicated by the collapse of the Kuomintang-Communist United Front and the cooperation between the Japanese army and the puppet government of Wang Jingwei.

Japan's occupation of Burma in 1942 severed China's critical supply lines. In response, the U.S. Army's Air Transport Command launched an operation called the Hump Airlift, flying vital supplies over the Himalayas from India to China. Flying over the Hump was a perilous and often suicidal mission for Allied flight crews, yet they were not alone in their struggle. The Chinese people and their army were always there, standing alongside the US forces. Chinese People helped build the US Air Force bases in China as well as airport ground handling work. Chinese pilots were sent to the United States for training and returned to form a groundbreaking team known as the China-US Air Force Mixed Formation.

This was not a traditional Chinese or U.S. Air Force unit, but a unique alliance, blending the strength of both nations' air forces. The pilots, side by side in the same fighter planes, fought together in the same war, united by a common cause. In the heat of battle, some American soldiers were saved by the Chinese, while others, having made the ultimate sacrifice, were laid to rest in China. This bond between the two nations, forged in the skies and on the ground, became a lasting symbol of shared bravery and mutual respect.

The U.S. Army's support continued even after Japan's surrender. They remained to oversee the safe surrender of Japanese forces and assist China in navigating the complex transition from war to peace. The cooperation between the two nations was unwavering, from start to finish.

Friendship and Culture Integration

During WWII in China, American and Chinese soldiers developed a strong bond through shared struggles and mutual respect. Though they came from different cultures, they worked together—building airfields, flying missions, and facing the challenges of war. Over time, they began to understand each other better, learning about each other's traditions and ways of life. It became normal for American soldiers to use chopsticks to eat their meals, and Chinese soldiers celebrated Christmas with the Americans. The Americans admired the Chinese for their resilience, while the Chinese respected the courage of the American soldiers. In the midst of conflict, this cultural exchange and friendship grew, showing how people from different backgrounds could come together to fight for a common cause.

American charity organizations provided essential support to civilians during the war, offering education, medical care, and food. Many of these organizations became places where different cultures blended. Chinese children, for example, found shelter in American-run orphanages in China, where they were kept safe and well cared for. These orphanages not only provided for their needs but also introduced them to Western traditions. The children learned English and celebrated holidays like Christmas, which brought some joy and a sense of normal life amidst the chaos of war.

Daily Life during the War Time

The political leadership demanded unwavering dedication to the war effort, placing daily life in the background. Yet, despite the chaos and uncertainty, people still had to find ways to work, eat, and care for their families. While fighting in China, American soldiers documented the daily realities of the Chinese people, capturing their observations and experiences through a unique lens. These accounts, rich in historical detail, offer invaluable insights for future generations. They not only tell the story of China during this tumultuous period but also honor the resilience and endurance of its people in the face of unimaginable hardship. In the meantime, the friendship of American and Chinese people.

In this book, we will explore photographs of everyday people in wartime China. These images, diverse and numerous, capture a wide range of individuals—from priests and soldiers to orphans, beggars, and ordinary civilians. These are people whose stories are often overlooked—those who laughed, cried, ate, drank, suffered, and sometimes thrived. The collection of pictures vividly brings to life the experiences of those who lived through this chaotic time.

引言

1931年9月18日，日軍炸毀滿洲境內鐵路並嫁禍給中國，以此為藉口展開侵略行動，史稱「九一八事變」。這次入侵行動後日本扶植成立傀儡政權「滿洲國」，中日雙方自此陷入長達十多年的戰爭狀態。起初戰爭僅限於一系列局部衝突，但在1937年盧溝橋事變之後中日全面開戰，太平洋戰爭又演變為二戰的一部分。從1937年到1945年為止，中日戰爭擾亂了千千萬萬百姓的生活，無數人為了求生存而痛苦掙扎，甚至有許多人缺乏食物和衣服等基本物資。在這一段期間，美國大眾從未忽略中國所遭遇的苦難。美國對中國的支持原本來自於民間，最終政府正式展開行動，整個過程中援助和團結的力量始終堅定不移。

民間援助

1930年代初期，不論是在中國還是其他地方，美國軍方都無法為進行中的戰事提供援助。有三個主要因素導致美國的參與度受限。首先，大蕭條嚴重影響了該國經濟，此時仍然在恢復過程當中。在資源捉襟見肘的情況下，國際上的衝突便非其優先考量。再者，許多美國人在第一次世界大戰之後深受和平主義和孤立主義的影響。歷經全球戰爭的恐怖與創傷後，國民不願再捲入另一場國外衝突，尤其是中國對他們來講實在太過遙遠。最後，當時美國正規部隊的規模實在太小，不足以應對國際上的需求。

儘管面臨重重挑戰，在強烈團結精神和道德責任感的驅使下，許多美國的私人基金會仍然集結起來支持中國的對日抗戰。他們的貢獻集中於醫療、教育和社會相關的倡議上，在美國政府官方援助有限的階段成為關鍵的希望來源。在許多美國慈善機構的支持下，孤兒院得以照顧難民兒童，並且設立醫院以滿足迫切的醫療需求，而學校的成立則是讓更多的中國民眾戰時仍有接受教育的機會。

1940年，許多這樣的機構聯合起來組成「美國援華聯合會」（American Federation to Aid China）。這個組織貢獻良多，包括教育美國公眾認識中國抗戰，並協助中國公共機構募款。除了提供物質上的支援外，該聯盟還致力於強化中美關係，強調中國迫切需要美國援助。他們所傳達的信息清晰有力：面對日本的侵略，中國正在孤軍奮戰。若無美國支援，恐將無以為繼。

經濟支援

二戰期間，美國向中國提供了大量經濟支援。1938年，中國以桐油作為抵押，從美國取得了2500萬美元的「桐油借款」，年息4.5厘，美方並限制這筆資金不得用於採購武器。1940年，中國又額外獲得了2000萬美元貸款，年息4厘，分七年償還。後來，在1940年10月，中國透過《鎢砂借款合約》獲得了2500萬元美元借款，在五年內用鎢砂償還。1941年簽訂的《中美金屬借款合約》允許中國向美國出售價值6000萬美元的礦物，以換取5000萬美元的貸款。這筆貸款有一半以現金支付，其餘專門用於購買美國的工農業產品。

1941年5月6日，小羅斯福總統宣布《租借法案》（Lend-Lease Act）將適用於中國，並指出「中國對美國國防至關重要，中國有資格獲得《租借法案》的援助。」大約一週過後，第一批價值110萬美元的《租借法案》物資就在5月18日從紐約運抵中國，其中包括300輛六輪卡車。美國透過《租借法案》向中國提供了大量的軍事援助，包括武器、飛機和彈藥。這樣的支援對於中國抗日戰爭至關重要，也有助於平民維持某種程度上的安穩生活。據美國歷史學家德懷特‧杜蒙（Dwight Dumond）估計，美國向中國提供的《租借法案》援助，截至1945年底總值為13.35億美元。

軍事合作

德國於1939年入侵波蘭，隨即與日本和義大利於1940年組成軸心國，而日本也開始入侵法屬印度支那。這一連串事件讓美國政府意識到，中國的戰事也與美國自身密切相關。1941年日本與蘇聯簽訂《日蘇中立條約》，情況變得更為急迫，該條約讓日本得以將部隊從滿洲和蒙古重新部署到其他地區，尤其是東南亞。

1941年，美國開始透過《租借法案》向中國提供財政和軍事支持，其中包括輸送軍事裝備和訓練中國軍官。中國透過這項計畫接收了100架P-40戰鬥機，美國陸軍飛行員也獲准離開崗位，前往中國協助作戰。這促成了飛虎隊的建立，而這支飛行員隊伍也是戰時美國支援中國對抗日軍的重要象徵。

　　1941年12月7日珍珠港事件之後，美國向日本宣戰，並與中國正式結盟。這促成了中緬印戰區（China Burma India Theater，簡稱 CBI）的建立，該戰區是二戰期間戰況最為激烈的地區之一。當時，日本已在中國部署了人數逾80萬的部隊，不論是地面部隊或是空中支援，配備的都是最新的武器。隨著第二次國共合作破局，以及日軍與汪精衛傀儡政府合作，中國內局勢變得更為詭譎。

　　日本於1942年佔領緬甸，切斷了中國的關鍵補給線。對此，美國陸軍空運司令部（U.S. Army's Air Transport Command）發起了名為「駝峰空運」（Hump Airlift）的行動，將重要物資從印度飛越喜瑪拉雅山脈運往中國。對於盟軍飛行員而言，飛越有如駝峰般的喜瑪拉雅山脈是極為危險的任務，經常無異於自殺，好在他們也並沒有獨自面對難關。中國的人民與軍隊時時刻刻支持著美軍，與他們並肩作戰。中國人協助美國空軍在中國興建基地，以及執行機場地勤工作。中國飛行員獲派前往美國受訓，並在回國後組成一支具有突破性的部隊，名為「中美空軍混合團」（China-US Air Force Mixed Formation）[1]。這並不單單是傳統意義上的中國或美國空軍部隊，而是一次獨特的盟軍組合，擷取了兩國空軍的長處。來自雙方的飛行員駕駛著同樣型號的戰機，在同一場戰爭裡並肩作戰，為了共同的目標而聯合在一起。在戰況最為激烈的時分，有些美國軍人被中國人營救，也有一些在捐軀後安葬於中國。兩國國民在天空中、在地面上建立了情誼，成為共同的勇氣與彼此間敬重的永恆象徵。

　　即使到了日本投降之後，美國陸軍仍然持續提供支援。他們留下來監督日軍投降的過程以確保安全，並協助中國走過從戰爭到和平的這段複雜過渡時期。兩國之間的合作自始至終屹立不搖。

---

1 正式英文名稱是 Chinese-American Composite Wing，簡稱 CACW。

友誼與文化融合

　　二戰期間，美、中兩國軍人在中國齊心協力、相互尊重，建立起堅固的情誼。雖然雙方文化背景不同，但他們一起建造機場、執行飛行任務，並面對戰爭的挑戰。他們逐漸了解彼此，學習對方的傳統和生活方式。美國軍人開始適應用筷子吃飯，中國軍人則與美軍一同慶祝聖誕節。美國人欽佩中國人的堅忍不拔，而中國人則敬重美國軍人的英勇武德。這樣的文化交流與友誼在烽火中不斷成長茁壯，展現出來自不同背景的人們如何團結起來為共同的理念奮鬥。

　　美國慈善組織在戰爭期間為平民提供了不可或缺的援助，包括教育、醫療和食物等方面。許多這一類組織也就形塑出不同文化交融的空間。例如，美國在華經營的孤兒院為許多中國兒童提供庇護，給予安全保障與細心照護。這些孤兒院不只滿足了他們的需求，也帶領他們認識西方傳統。孩子們學習英語並慶祝聖誕節等節日，在混沌不明的戰爭局勢中帶來了些許歡愉，彷彿生活又回歸了正常。

戰時日常生活

　　政府高層要求人民將日常生活擱置一旁，堅定不移地為了戰爭而奉獻。然而，儘管日常充斥著混沌與無常，人們仍然必須想辦法工作、吃飯還有養家糊口。在華作戰期間，許多美國軍人記錄了中國人民的日常現實，透過獨特的鏡頭捕捉他們的觀察和經驗。這些寶貴的紀錄充滿豐富的歷史細節，也讓後代得以洞察當時的真實生活。他們拍的相片不僅將中國在這個動盪時期的故事娓娓道來，也彰顯出中國人民如何面對難以想像的困境，將韌性和耐力發揮到極致。與此同時，這些故事也講述了中美兩國人民之間日益滋長的友誼。

　　他們為戰時中國民眾拍了哪些日常生活照片呢？這就是本書要探究的主題。那些五花八門且為數眾多的照片捕捉了中國的眾生相，有神父與士兵，也有孤兒、乞丐以及一般老百姓。這些人的故事經常遭到忽視——他們笑過、哭過、受苦過，偶爾能吃喝享樂，也有欣欣向榮的時刻。在這些照片中，歷經戰時混亂生活的老百姓們可說是栩栩如生。

WARTIME
REFUGEES

The Second Sino-Japanese war, between 1937 and 1945, triggered China's largest instance of forced movement ever. Refugees fled in record numbers from the encroaching Japanese army. Because the Japanese invasion primarily came from the coast, refugees generally fled from northern and eastern regions such as Beijing, Tianjin, Shanghai, and Nanjing towards southern and western ones such as Sichuan, Yunnan, and Guizhou. News of Japanese massacres such as the Nanjing massacre, as well as the terror created by bombing raids, caused waves of refugees to form, as people panicked and fled the violence.

Modes of travel

Refugees needed a way to get to their destination, wherever they went. Many who could not afford other means of transportation traveled on foot, enduring harsh conditions over long distances. The open roads exposed refugees to unforgiving weather conditions while they walked long distances, leading to many deaths. Oftentimes, people walked because there were problems with the trains. Railway infrastructure was often destroyed or otherwise unavailable, and many did not have the money to pay for train tickets or other forms of transportation such as carts or rickshaws. The terrible conditions over the roads led to many deaths. There was inadequate food supplies and medical care, leading to rampant malnutrition and epidemics. According to *In a Sea of Bitterness*, a cholera epidemic in Shaoxing in 1940 had a mortality rate of almost 25%. Refugees fleeing to the countryside lacked professional medical care, and many people died from otherwise curable illnesses. Once refugees arrived at refugee camps, their troubles weren't over. Relief systems were not equipped to deal with the massive influx of refugees, causing deaths from starvation and sickness as food and medical supplies ran out.

The preferred overland travel method was by train, mainly because it was much quicker than walking. This wasn't a safe travel method either, as trains were frequently overcrowded due to high demand. Desperate to escape the Japanese, people clung to the sides of trains and sat on the front, occupying areas not designed for passengers. As a result, many people died by falling from moving trains, sometimes into the train's wheels. Rivers and sea routes were also crucial for refugee movement. Rivers such as the Yangzi offered safer, faster routes than overland travel, particularly for those fleeing China to the West. Travel by boat had its own dangers, particularly that of overcrowded boats capsizing. Pirates and Japanese patrols also posed threats to maritime routes.

Some refugees such as peasants didn't travel far. Their livelihoods were tied to their land, and they didn't have much money, so they often couldn't leave. Instead, they fled to safer areas nearby when fighting reached them, returning when fighting had cooled down. Sometimes, combat restarted and they became refugees again. Other refugees, though, traveled great distances, such as across provinces, in order to escape danger. The influx of refugees in inland provinces strained local resources, leading to problems such as overcrowding, food shortages, and disease outbreaks. There were also great disruptions to social structures and the economy due to chaos caused by the war. At the same time, the refugee movement also caused talented people and specialists to group up in cities, helping the war effort and leading to development in some areas. Finally, some refugees fled to neutral territory, such as Hong Kong and Macau. Others took ships to Vietnam, Burma, and Southeast Asia. This offered relative safety from the Japanese, but it impacted the social and economic structures of the host territories, leading to the same effects as the increased population density in inland areas of China.

Effects of refugee movement

The hordes of refugees moving inland put massive strain on existing food and water supplies. During the war, the food supply was already limited due to shortages and transportation disruptions. For example, according to *In a Sea of Bitterness*, Zhejiang farmers were already about 14 million piculs short of feeding the entire province. The shortfall was supplemented by imports from other areas, but food transportation networks may have been disrupted by the war. During the war, the "rice basket" of the region, northern Zhejiang, was almost entirely occupied by the Japanese. In Jinhua, all of the refugee food supplies in the province were exhausted, leading to refugees subsisting on tree bark and grass roots. The only answer was forcing the refugees out of Jinhua. In high mountain villages, there were severe water shortages, often leading to outbreaks of diseases such as dysentery.

Inland cities were usually not prepared to deal with the flood of refugees, and the crisis quickly overwhelmed existing housing. People slept wherever they could, such as in office corridors, stockrooms, and warehouses. In refugee camps, many different people from different areas of China were all forced to live and interact with one another. In this way, the lack of housing helped bring urban and rural life together very effectively.

Rural areas often didn't have much extra shelter set up, so refugees often had to rely on makeshift accommodations or ask families to host them. Special facilities such as state-run orphanages and care centers were set up for orphaned and/or displaced children.

Due to overcrowding, poor living conditions, and lack of adequate medical care, refugee populations were very prone to epidemics. In Shaoxing in 1940, a cholera outbreak infected 5,674 thousand people, with a mortality rate close to 25% (also used in previous writing). An epidemic of Bubonic plague in Yiwu County was started by infected travelers. Out of 682 people infected, 630 of them died, a death rate of over 90%.

Refugee camps were usually crowded and unsanitary, which was compounded by inadequate medical resources and infrastructure. Being a refugee was tough on the body, weakening the immune system, with diseases such as Malaria and Dysentery being all too common. All these factors fostered the spread of diseases. At a refugee reception center in Wuxi, the area was described as crowded, with over 100 people packed together. The air smelled thick and dirty. Refugees from the battle for Shanghai and the Japanese carpet bombing of Zhabei fled to the 10 square miles of the French Concession and International Settlement, more than doubling the population to 4 million. There was simply not enough housing, and winter caused over 100,000 people to die from factors such as disease, exposure, and starvation.

Some epidemics were not caused by nature, but instead by the Japanese. Japanese planes flew over Quzhou and Ningbo in 1940, carrying parcels of grain and bubonic plague infested fleas. In Quzhou, within eight weeks, 21 out of 22 people died, and in 1941, 275 of 281 infected people died. tens of thousands of people fled, spreading the plague even further. Around Quzhou, the plague killed over 2,000 people. In Ningbo, the plague was washed into drinking water from the rain. By the end of the year, 106 people had died, including twelve whole families. The plague was eventually contained via a quarantine that displaced hundreds. The area was then burned to the ground to eliminate the plague for good. The plague had a staggering death rate, with over 90% of those infected dying.

Children

Children were often separated from or left without parents in the chaos of the Japanese invasion and refugee movements. This caused the amount of orphans to swell. For example, the number of orphanages in Sichuan, Guizhou, Guangxi, Fujian, Jiangxi, Guangdong, Hong Kong, Zhejiang, Shaanxi, and Gansu grew from 28 in 1938 to 61.

Many families were split up during bombing raids or evacuations. Other times, children and elderly family members were abandoned or seriously neglected on purpose. When children were too tired to move, they were often left on the road to die. While separated families were sometimes able to reunite, the fear of never seeing one another again loomed heavily over refugees. Many Chinese refugees fled to other countries, but got stuck and were unable to return for a while. After the war, family members sometimes randomly bumped into each other in often unexpected places. However, not all reunions were joyful. Many times, relatives had been completely changed by the war.

Special refugees

The Nanjing Massacre in December 1937 caused one of the biggest refugee crises of the Sino-Japanese War. As Japanese soldiers attacked the city and committed terrible atrocities, hundreds of thousands of people fled for their lives. In Nanjing alone, over 335,000 people were forced to leave their homes. Many refugees headed west to cities like Wuhan, which quickly became overcrowded. For example, Wuhan's population grew from 1 million to 1.5 million in just a few months, leading to serious housing and food shortages.

It wasn't just Chinese citizens who were refugees; There were also 20,000 stateless Jews. These Jews fled to Shanghai from between 1933 and 1941 in order to escape Nazi Germany. In 1941, Shanghai was captured by the Japanese. Japan was allied with Nazi Germany, so the Jews were rounded up in a ghetto at Tilanqiao. Conditions in the ghetto were less than ideal, but residents made the most of it, maintaining Jewish life with traditions such as theater and music. In the end, the majority of Shanghai's Jews survived, mainly because they weren't main targets for the Japanese.

The 1942 Henan famine, caused by a combination of natural disasters and wartime requisitions, led to one of the largest refugee crises during the Sino-Japanese War. Over three million people died, while another three to four million fled their homes. The famine was triggered by failed spring and summer rains, followed by a locust infestation that destroyed the harvest. Compounding the crisis, the frontlines of the war cut off Henan from outside aid, and local authorities were unable to release grain from granaries, as it was already going to the military. The lack of relief efforts left the people of Henan with two choices: flee or die.

Refugees endured harrowing conditions. Some sold family members into servitude or prostitution in a desperate bid for survival. For example, in several places, "human markets" emerged, where daughters were sold to buyers. In some villages, famine victims resorted to eating bark, peanut shells, and even earth, leading to poisoning and death. In Sishui, the population fell from 95,000 to 61,600, with 30,000 fleeing and 3,400 dying of hunger. Meanwhile, urban centers like Zhengzhou were devastated, with the population plummeting from 120,000 to less than 40,000 due to famine and Japanese bombardment.

Relief attempts

The central government played a critical role in establishing the framework for refugee relief. Policies were created to distribute daily financial aid, food, and travel allowances. However, implementation was often challenging due to limited resources and dependency on local governments. The government sought to centralize relief efforts, acknowledging the critical need for food and financial support. However, reliance on local funding sources, such as increased taxation or forced contributions, created tension within already struggling communities. This highlights a fundamental limitation of wartime governance: while policies might be ambitious, resource constraints often reduced their impact on the ground.

Wuhan, as a key strategic city, became a focal point for refugee relief. Municipal authorities collaborated with national agencies to establish shelters and provide basic necessities. However, the sheer volume of refugees overwhelmed these efforts. The scale of displacement in Wuhan during the war was staggering, with hundreds of thousands of refugees arriving after the fall of Nanjing and other cities. The city's response demonstrates the complexity of coordinating relief efforts in an urban environment under siege. Despite setting up shelters, overcrowding, inadequate medical care, and shortages of food and water plagued the system. Temporary housing was critical in urban centers to accommodate the displaced. Refugee shelters were often improvised, utilizing public buildings, warehouses, and even private homes. However, these spaces were not designed for long-term habitation, leading to significant challenges. Refugee shelters became hubs of both relief and suffering. While they provided immediate safety, the lack of proper sanitation, healthcare, and adequate living space turned these shelters into sites of vulnerability. Diseases such as cholera and dysentery spread rapidly, particularly in the absence of medical infrastructure.

Providing food to displaced populations was a cornerstone of refugee relief efforts. Despite prioritizing food security, the government faced logistical challenges and frequent delays. Food shortages exposed the fragility of wartime supply chains. Refugees frequently endured hunger due to delayed shipments or mismanagement. Corruption further eroded trust in relief systems, with resources sometimes diverted or stolen. This added a layer of social tension, as vulnerable populations often felt abandoned by the state.

International aid groups tried to set up operations in China in order to help deal with the refugee crisis. For example, the Red Cross provided critical support, such as organizing refugee shelters and distributing medical supplies. However, it simply could not do enough in the face of such an extreme and widespread crisis. Missionaries, particularly Christian organizations, played a vital role in refugee relief. They set up soup kitchens, schools, and shelters for displaced individuals. These played a significant but limited role, as while they provided critical relief to thousands, financial exhaustion often curtailed their operations. Founded in the 1920s, the Red Swastika society was a benevolent association modeled off of the red cross. Throughout the war, they tried to help wherever they could. For example, early in the war, they became known for burying unclaimed bodies on the streets of Nanjing. In 1937, they established 10 refugee reception centers and a temporary hospital, and in 1938, they joined the Ahejiang Refugee Relief Society. Their main goal for dealing with refugees was to get them to a further area or to return them home if the area was safe.

Local Communities often banded together to shore up support for refugees. They played a crucial role in housing and feeding refugees, whether at their final destination or a stop on their journey. Despite their own challenges, such as struggles to find food and money, villagers welcomed refugees into their homes, showcasing a remarkable sense of solidarity during this time of crisis. People helped each other because everyone was affected by the invasion, creating a shared bond. Local Relief Councils were instrumental in managing refugee reception centers and distributing food and supplies. They were often the first line of support for displaced populations, seeking contributions from residents and negotiating with the central government for additional resources. Communities worked together to raise funds and coordinate volunteer efforts. There were still many problems, though. The economy was terrible, so nobody had much money, food, or room to spare for refugees. Some people were bitter at what they perceived as refugees using up supplies that were theirs.

Many challenges prevented the flow of aid to refugees. These included effects from the war, such as destroyed railways, the danger of bombing, and general chaos. Corruption and inefficiency also undermined many programs, causing aid to be delayed or misallocated.

戰時難民

1937 年至 1945 年的中國抗日戰爭引發了中國史上最大規模的強制遷徙。隨著日軍步步進逼，被迫逃亡的難民人數前所未見。由於日本主要由沿海地區展開入侵行動，難民大致上由北平[1]、天津、上海、南京等華北與華東地區逃往中國西南部的四川、雲貴等地區。隨著南京大屠殺等日軍暴行的消息傳開，以及狂轟濫炸所造成的恐慌，使得人們倉皇逃離暴力，引發了一波又一波的難民潮。

移動模式

　　難民無論要去哪裡，總得要想辦法到達目的地。許多人無法負擔搭乘其他交通工具的費用而選擇徒步移動，一路上他們被迫忍受嚴酷的環境。野外的道路讓難民在長途跋涉時暴露在嚴苛的天氣中，死難者不計其數。人們也常因為火車故障等狀況而選擇走路。鐵路的相關基礎設施經常由於受到破壞或是其他緣故而無法使用，而許多人也無力支付火車票或其他交通工具的費用，例如馬車或人力車。沿路的狀況惡劣，導致許多人死亡。食物供應和醫療照護不足，導致營養不良的情形和流行病猖獗。根據美國史家蕭邦齊（R. Keith Schoppa）的著作《苦海求生：抗戰時期的中國難民》（*In a Sea of Bitterness: Refugees during the Sino-Japanese War*），紹興於 1940 年爆發霍亂疫情，死亡率接近 25%。逃往農村的難民缺乏專業醫療照護，其中許多人死於理應可以治癒的疾病。即使難民終於抵達難民營，他們的苦難還沒到盡頭。救濟系統的設施無法應付大量湧入的難民，隨著食物和醫療用品耗盡，導致人們因飢餓與疾病而死亡。

　　陸路移動的首選方式是搭乘火車，主要是因為火車比步行快得多。由於需求量大，火車經常擁擠不堪，使得這種移動方式也不安全。為了逃離日軍，人們會緊抓火車兩側，或是坐在車頭上等等，這些不適合載客的區域也都擠滿了人。結果許多人就在火車行駛過程中墜落罹難，有時甚至遭捲入火車的輪子裡。河流和海路也是難民遷徙的關鍵路線。特

1　1949 年 10 月 1 日中華人民共和國成立後，北平再度改稱北京。

別是對於那些從中國逃往西方的人們來說，長江等河流構成的路線是比陸路更為安全、快速。乘船移動自有其危險性，尤其是過度擁擠的船隻容易翻覆。海盜和日本巡邏艇也對海上航線構成了威脅。

某些難民並沒有移動得太遠，例如農民。他們的生計與自己的土地息息相關，而且也沒有多少錢，所以他們往往無法離開。他們只有在戰火迫在眉睫時，才會逃到附近較為安全的地方，等到局勢緩和後再返回。有時候，戰鬥再次爆發，他們又成為難民。其他難民則為了逃避危險而長途跋涉，例如跨省移動。大量難民湧入內陸省份，使當地資源吃緊，進一步衍生人滿為患、糧食短缺和疾病爆發等問題。社會結構與經濟也由於戰爭造成的混亂而嚴重受損。與此同時，難民的遷徙也使人才和專家匯聚在大後方的一些城市，為戰爭貢獻心力，反而促進部分地區的發展。最後，有些難民逃往中立地區，例如香港和澳門。另一些難民則乘船前往越南、緬甸和東南亞。這對於躲避日軍威脅是相對安全的選項，但卻影響了收容地的社會和經濟結構，導致這些國家跟中國內陸地區一樣，因為人口密度增加而飽受衝擊。

難民遷徙的影響

成群的難民湧向內陸，為食物與用水供應帶來巨大挑戰。戰爭期間，由於糧食短缺和交通中斷，糧食供應已經十分有限。舉例來說，根據《苦海求生》一書所述，浙江農民此時所生產的糧食已經不足以養活全省，足足少了1400萬擔的米糧。短缺的糧食由其他地區進口補足，但糧食運輸網絡可能已因戰爭而中斷。戰爭期間，浙江北部作為該地區的糧倉，幾乎完全遭日軍佔領。在金華，省內所有供應給難民的糧食皆已耗盡，導致難民只能以樹皮和草根糊口。唯一的解決辦法就是把難民趕出金華。高山村落嚴重缺水，往往導致痢疾等疾病爆發。

內陸城市通常沒有做好應對大量難民的準備，這場危機迅速讓現有的住房情形左支右絀。人們睡在辦公室走廊、貯藏室和倉庫等任何有辦法睡覺的地方。在難民營裡，許多來自中國不同地區的人被迫住在一起，與彼此互動。這樣一來，住房的匱乏反倒是非常有助於城市和農村生活的高度融合。

　　農村地區往往沒有太多額外的收容所，所以難民通常只能依靠臨時搭建的住所或是請求農家收容。國營孤兒院和照護中心等特殊設施所收留的則是孤兒或流離失所的兒童，抑或兩者都有。

　　由於過度擁擠、生活條件惡劣又缺乏足夠的醫療照顧，難民很容易受到流行病的侵襲。如前所述，1940 年紹興霍亂疫情的死亡率接近 25%，導致 567.4 萬人遭感染。義烏縣的鼠疫疫情則是由受感染的移入者引發。在 682 名感染者中，有 630 人死亡，死亡率超過 90%。

　　難民營通常擁擠不堪且不衛生，加上醫療資源和基礎設施不足，使情況更加惡劣。難民往往因為顛沛流離而出現各種身體問題，除了會削弱免疫系統，瘧疾和痢疾等疾病實在過於普遍。這些因素都助長了疾病的傳播。據悉，無錫某個收容難民的地方甚為擁擠，有超過 100 人擠在一個小空間裡。空氣中散發著濃濁的污穢氣味。淞滬會戰和日軍對閘北展開地毯式轟炸期間，湧入的難民潮導致僅僅 10 平方英里大的法租界和公共租界人口增加了一倍多，達到 400 萬。當時根本沒有足夠的住房，寒冬造成超過 10 萬人死於疾病、凍傷和飢餓。

　　有些流行病並非自然引起，而是日本人刻意造成的。1940 年，日軍飛機飛過了衢州和寧波上空。這些飛機運載著穀物包裹，裡面帶有感染了鼠疫的跳蚤。在衢州，八週內受感染的 22 人中有 21 人死亡，而到了 1941 年，281 名感染者中有 275 人死亡。數以萬計居民逃往外地，導致瘟疫進一步蔓延。在衢州周圍，鼠疫造成 2000 多人死亡。在寧波，雨水沖刷讓鼠疫病原污染了飲用水。截至年底，已有 106 人死亡，其中包括 12 戶家庭。最終透過隔離才控制住疫情，數以百計居民因此流離失所。該地區隨後被徹底焚毀，以永久消滅鼠疫。這場瘟疫的死亡率極為驚人，有超過 90% 的感染者死亡。

兒童

在日本入侵和難民遷徙的一片混亂之中,許多兒童與父母失散或是失去了雙親。這導致了孤兒的人數激增。例如,四川、貴州、廣西、福建、江西、廣東、香港、浙江、陝西和甘肅等省份的孤兒院數量從 1938 年的 28 間增加到 61 間。

許多家庭在空襲或疏散期間被拆散。也有一些家庭刻意遺棄兒童和老人,或對他們疏於照顧。如果孩子們太累而無法移動,他們經常會被拋棄在路上等死。雖然失散的家庭有時能夠團聚,但再也見不到彼此的恐懼卻深深地籠罩著難民。許多中國難民逃到其他國家,但卻一時無法返國,陷入困境。許多人有時會在意想不到的地方與家人偶然重聚。然而,並非所有的團聚都充滿著喜悅。很多時候,家屬們早已因為戰爭而徹底改變。

特殊的難民

抗戰期間衍生的重大難民危機甚多,1937 年 12 月的南京大屠殺是其中之一。隨著日本士兵攻打這座城市並犯下駭人聽聞的暴行,數十萬南京人逃亡保命。僅僅南京一地,就有超過 33.5 萬人被迫逃離家園。許多難民向西逃往武漢等城市,但那些地方很快便人滿為患。例如,武漢的人口在短短幾個月內從 100 萬增加為 150 萬,導致住房和食物嚴重短缺。

成為難民的不僅僅是中國公民而已,還有 2 萬名無國籍猶太人。這些猶太人在 1933 年至 1941 年間為了逃離納粹德國而逃到上海。日本於 1941 年占領整個上海後,因為日本是納粹德國的盟友,猶太人被集中到位於提籃橋的猶太人隔都(ghetto)。隔都的環境並不理想,但是居民盡可能享受生活,透過戲劇和音樂等維持猶太人的傳統生活方式。最終,上海的大多數猶太人都得以倖存,主因是他們並非日本人的首要迫害目標。

1942年的河南大饑荒由天災和戰時政府對各種民間資源的徵用共同造成，引發了抗戰期間最大的難民危機之一。罹難人數超過300萬，另有300至400萬人逃離家園。由於春季和夏季的雨水不足，繼而蝗蟲肆虐破壞收成，引發了饑荒。戰爭的前線隔絕了河南的外援，加劇了危機；地方政府無法開放糧倉發放糧食，因為早已遭軍隊徵用一空。河南人在缺乏救濟援助的情形下只有兩種選擇：不是逃難，就是等死。

　　難民們經歷了悲慘的處境。有些人為了在絕境中生存，不惜將家人賣為奴僕或是娼妓。例如，在幾個地方出現了「人口市場」，許多人在此公開出售自己的女兒。在某些村莊，饑荒災民只能吃樹皮、花生殼，甚至是泥土，導致他們因此中毒，甚至死亡。在山東泗水，隨著3萬人出逃與3400人死於饑荒，當地人口從9.5萬降為6.16萬。與此同時，鄭州等城市也遭到破壞；由於饑荒和日軍轟炸，人口從12萬銳減到4萬以下。

綁手綁腳的救濟行動

　　中央政府在建立難民救濟框架方面發揮了關鍵作用。各機關制定了政策來分配日常的經濟援助、食物和交通津貼。然而，由於資源有限且必須依賴於地方政府，實際執行起來往往困難重重。政府意識到對於糧食和經濟支援的迫切需求，試圖讓救濟工作由中央統籌。然而，對於地方資金來源的依賴，例如增加稅收或是強制性捐獻，讓已經陷入困境的社群更為緊繃。這突顯了戰時治理在根本上的局限性：儘管政策在制訂上可能有雄心壯志，但是對於地方的實際影響往往因為資源有限而大打折扣。

　　武漢是重要的戰略城市，也成為救助難民的重鎮。市政府嘗試與中央機構合作建立收容所，並提供基本的生活必需品。但這仍然難以應付龐大的難民人數。戰爭期間，武漢流離失所的規模相當驚人，在南京和其他城市陷落後，有數十萬難民抵達該地。透過武漢採取的應變措施，我們可以看到，在遭到圍困的城市環境中協調救援工作是何等複雜。儘管設置了收容所，但整個系統仍然受到過度擁擠、醫療照護不足以及食物和水資源短缺等問題困擾。在市中心，臨時住所對於安置流離失所的人們至關重要。難民收容所通常是利用公共建物、倉庫，甚至是私人住宅臨時搭建而成。然而，這些空間並非提供長期居住使用，這也帶來了重大挑戰。難民收容所救濟了許多人，但同時也讓他們受苦。儘管難民收容所提供了即時的安全保障，但由於缺乏適當的衛生措施、醫療保健和充足的生活空間，這些收容所變成了疾病橫行的地方。尤其是在缺乏醫療基礎設施的情況下，霍亂和痢疾等疾病迅速蔓延。

為流離失所的人們提供糧食是難民救援工作的根本。儘管政府優先考慮糧食安全，但他們仍然面臨後勤方面的挑戰和頻繁的延誤。糧食短缺暴露了戰時供應鏈的脆弱。由於運輸延誤或管理不善，難民經常挨餓。資源遭挪用或竊占的情形也時有所聞，貪腐進一步削弱了人們對於救濟系統的信任。在弱勢群體經常感到被國家拋棄的情形下，社會的緊張態勢更形加劇。

國際援助組織嘗試在中國開展業務，以幫助應對難民危機。例如，紅十字會提供了重要支援，如籌劃難民收容所和分發醫療用品。然而，面對如此無所不在的極端危機，紅十字會能做的實在不多。傳教士、尤其是基督宗教組織在救濟難民時發揮了至關重要的作用。他們為流離失所的人們設立了慈善廚房、學校和收容所。數以千計難民能獲得救濟，這些設施扮演重要角色，但也常因財源枯竭而導致成效有限。仿效紅十字會的慈善組織「世界紅卍字會」成立於1920年代。從抗戰開始到最後，他們嘗試盡其所能提供援助。例如，在戰爭初期，他們因為幫忙埋葬南京街頭無人認領的屍體而聞名。1937年，他們設立了10個難民接待中心和一間臨時醫院，並於1938年加入了浙江省難民救濟協會。他們應對難民的主要目標是把他們送到下一個地方，或是協助他們在家鄉安全的情形下返家。

地方上的社群經常聯合起來支援難民。這些地方無論是難民的最終目的地，抑或只是路途上的停靠點，難民能有地方吃住都是靠地方居民的重要貢獻。即使村民們面臨著諸如缺乏糧食與資金來源等方面的挑戰，他們還是歡迎難民住進自己家裡，在如此危難時分展現了非凡的團結精神。因為每個人都受到了侵略的影響，人們相互扶持而展現出同仇敵愾的同胞愛。地方上的救濟委員會在管理難民接待中心、分配糧食和物資等方面大有助益。在援助流離失所人口的工作方面，這類組織往往能站上第一線；他們向居民募款，並與中央政府協商以獲得額外資源。社群同心協力募集資金並協調志工的工作。但是他們仍然面臨不少問題。由於經濟體系崩潰，沒有人能夠提供多餘的金錢、糧食或是居住空間給難民。有些人因為自己的物資遭難民佔用而心生怨懟。

　　援助難民的工作遭逢重重阻礙。其中包括戰爭所帶來的影響，例如鐵路遭毀壞、面臨空襲，還有戰亂時的各種問題。貪腐和效率低下也破壞了許多計畫，導致這些援助被拖延或是分配不當。

A mother crying over her son, who fell from a moving train and died.

一個男孩從行進中的火車上墜落而死去,母親在其身旁放聲痛哭。

Date of Photo 時間:November 10, 1944
Credits 來源:美國國家檔案館 Photo Courtesy of National Archives

Chinese refugees resting at a train stop.

一群在火車站休息的中國難民。

Date of Photo 時間：November 10, 1944
Credits 來源：美國國家檔案館 Photo Courtesy of National Archives

Refugees resting in the wheels of a parked train.

難民在一列靜止的火車的輪子間休息。

Date of Photo 時間：November 10, 1944
Credits 來源：美國國家檔案館 Photo Courtesy of National Archives

As the train stops at a station, refugees immediately rush to pick up hot ashes to use as heating.

列車一到站，難民便馬上搶著拾取熱灰，以便用於加熱或取暖。

Date of Photo 時間：November 10, 1944
Credits 來源：美國國家檔案館 Photo Courtesy of National Archives

A Chinese family resting under a makeshift shelter at a railway stop.

一個中國家庭在車站裡臨時搭建的遮蔽處裡休息。

Date of Photo 時間：November 10, 1944
Credits 來源：美國國家檔案館 Photo Courtesy of National Archives

Chinese refugees fleeing from the Japanese with retreating soldiers.

中國難民與撤退的部隊一同逃離日軍。

Date of Photo 時間：November 10, 1944
Credits 來源：美國國家檔案館 Photo Courtesy of National Archives

Refugees packing onto every square foot of a moving train in order to escape the Japanese

難民為了逃離日軍,擠滿了行進間火車上的每一寸空間。

Date of Photo 時間:November 10, 1944
Credits 來源:美國國家檔案館 Photo Courtesy of National Archives

A refugee with two children, one of whom has his head bandaged.
一位帶著兩個孩子的難民,其中一位頭上綁著繃帶。

Date of Photo 時間:November 10, 1944
Credits 來源:美國國家檔案館 Photo Courtesy of National Archives

Two refugee children trying to get some rest before they have to move again.

因為暫時不用上路逃難,兩個難民兒童藉機稍事休息。

Date of Photo 時間:November 10, 1944
Credits 來源:美國國家檔案館 Photo Courtesy of National Archives

Refugees carrying their packs while walking along a railroad line.

難民們扛著家當,沿著鐵路前行。

Date of Photo 時間:November 10, 1944
Credits 來源:美國國家檔案館 Photo Courtesy of National Archives

A refugee suffering from malnutrition.
一位因為營養不良而骨瘦如柴的難民。

Date of Photo 時間：November 10, 1944
Credits 來源：美國國家檔案館 Photo Courtesy of National Archives

WOMEN AND
CHILDREN

Women and jobs

During the Second Sino-Japanese war and the subsequent occupation, China underwent severe hyperinflation and economic turmoil, resulting in a piss poor economy. The Beijing economy plunged during the Japanese occupation, as the regime didn't have much money, and much of the money they did have was spent on police forces. Government workers at institutions such as schools had their wages nearly frozen, meaning their incomes couldn't keep up with inflation. The handicraft industries had employed women in large and small ways, but when Western tourists and markets left, the industry crashed. This flipped the social order on its head, as there was a sudden increase in female wage earners. Before the war, the city had a very small female workforce. By 1936, however, conditions had changed and 7.6% of Beijing's female population were wage earners. Unmarried women tended to have better times finding work than married women, due to fewer obligations. The amount of informal, part time work, such as Chinese tutoring, among women increased as well. One sector that helped prop up the Chinese economy was the service sector. Service jobs had a large customer base, as they served Chinese civilians and newly arrived Japanese civilians. Two jobs that had a large increase in female workers after the war began were as part of the police and as a typist. One main reason for the inclusion of women into the police force was the ability for policewomen to conduct body searches on other women. Male criminals often used women to conduct crimes, so having policewomen to frisk women in public spaces would help decrease crime. The social acceptance of policewomen also allowed the Japanese regime to enforce tighter security. The main goal of Beijing's female police force became to frisk women and children, as well as checking their luggage at city gates and railroad stations. The pay wasn't that great; At 30 yen, it was about half that of an elementary school teacher, though the police did get small, regular salary boosts. While there was some resistance to change, some men acknowledged the need for women to work. A Qingdao man wrote that everyone had an obligation to serve society, and elders needed to see that women working outside of the home was honorable, not reputation ruining.

The New Life Movement

The New Life Movement was created in 1934 by Chiang Kai-shek and his wife, Song Meiling, to fix what they perceived as a loss of traditional values, and to prepare China for modernization and war. Chiang firmly believed that China needed spiritual strength to defeat the more industrialized Japanese. He believed that if China had "military valor", they wouldn't need to rely on weapons, and the Japanese would be unable to destroy the "strength of spirit" generated by it. The New Life Movement was then created to discipline and train people to become model citizens, giving China this "strength of spirit". One foundational activity of the New Life Movement was teaching better hygiene practices and encouraging discipline in one's daily life. The movement also sought to educate citizens on nationalistic values and personal improvement, involving propaganda, including slogans and guidelines for better living. For example, people were encouraged to dress frugally, with men in Chongqing wearing military uniforms or suits, and women wearing simple cotton gowns. Furthermore, propaganda such as the "Citizens' Pledge" was required to be posted at all teahouses during the war. These pledges included points such as vowing never to help traitors, never to disobey the government, and never to surrender. The denouncement of traitors was also used to persecute anyone who challenged the government's authority. Women were a major part of the movement, as they were seen as the ones who could keep families and society strong. The movement also encouraged women to wear modest clothes, stay clean, and avoid being flashy. Groups like the Women's Advisory Council taught women about how they could contribute to society by being good caregivers and staying loyal to the nation. Finally, the New Life Movement encouraged individual improvement by tying it to larger national goals. Citizens were encouraged to align their behavior with the country's needs, especially now that it was in a war. While the program was criticized for focusing on minor moral reforms over deeper systemic issues, it had several long lasting achievements in Chinese history. It reinforced self-discipline and spread Confucian values. It helped improve hygiene and spread public health awareness, helping control the spread of disease and improving sanitation. Furthermore, it helped mobilize the Chinese people for war by instilling a sense of national responsibility.

Changing societal expectations

During the war, traditional employment was shaken up. Traditional Confucian values that emphasized women's roles as wives and mothers were challenged by the demands of the war. Economic hardship and shifting societal norms led to an increase in women's participation in the education sector. *Women's Journal,* a Beijing publication during the war, reflected these shifts. While women were initially encouraged to prioritize domestic roles, the worsening economy led to an acceptance of women in education and other forms of employment. Due to the terrible economy, many young women had to withdraw from school in order to find jobs and support their families. Women were often subject to sexual harassment, lower wages, and job discrimination while also being expected to support their families. Unlike in many Western countries such as America, the wartime gains made by women in China stuck around long after the war. The CCP(Chinese Communist Party) won the civil war after WWII, which helped due to the communist insistence on equality between men and women, along with the necessity for women to work. Oftentimes, widows were the sole breadwinners for them and their children. As higher education expanded during the war, a growing number of young women began to work beyond their hometowns and regions. The disruptions to the social order caused by the war were so large, a postwar return to prewar norms was inconceivable.

Children in the war

The war was obviously not a good place to be a child in. Many children were forced to flee from the Japanese army, live in poverty, or endure separation from their parents. For many, childhood meant constant movement and struggle for survival. Children were often forced to work in order to support their families. During the chaotic flight of refugee families, many children were separated from their parents, forcing them to navigate the horrors of war on their own. Many families had to march for weeks or months to find safety. As a result, Elderly family members and Children who were not able to keep up with the pace of the rest of their family were sometimes left on the side of the road to die. Constantly on the run, many children were not able to receive a proper education or even settle down and rest. Due to a crisis in housing, families were forced to raise their children in cramped, unsanitary homes. With the extra required furniture such as chamber pots, crates, and beds, it was said that pavilion rooms, a cheap yet small type of living space, felt like warehouses due to their crowded nature.

Despite the hardships of the war, children found joy in sports, performances, and community activities. Traditional games, storytelling, and communal activities provided brief respites from the chaos. These activities also helped preserve cultural identity and fostered a sense of normalcy. Children often interacted with the army during the war. For example, children gave plays to soldiers, and soldiers were sometimes asked to give military training to schools, focusing on drills and marksmanship. In some areas, puppet shows and local theater performances were organized to entertain children, subtly incorporating patriotic themes to bolster morale and resistance against the occupiers.

During WWII, after the attack on Pearl Harbor, the US stationed soldiers in China to help combat the Japanese. These soldiers encountered various Chinese children in different circumstances. These interactions ranged from providing humanitarian aid and friendship to informal educational exchanges. American soldiers helped offer food, protection, and emotional support to many war-affected children, giving them some stability in a decidedly unstable time. They often distributed candies and food rations to these children, making them figures of admiration. In some cases, US military officers worked with local Chinese governments to provide aid to refugee children. American soldiers also taught English words and Western games to Chinese children, causing some Chinese children to pick up English phrases and mimic American mannerisms.

戰時婦孺

婦女與工作

　　對日抗戰拉開序幕後，中國許多地方遭佔領，國內歷經嚴重的惡性通貨膨脹和經濟動盪，導致經濟崩盤。日本在佔領期間扶持的政權並沒有多少資金，且僅有的經費大都用於維持警力，這使得北平的經濟嚴重衰退。任職於學校等機構的公務員之工資幾乎全面凍漲，這意味著他們的收入跟不上通貨膨脹。手工業曾經以大大小小的各種方式僱用婦女，但是西方遊客一離開就沒了市場，這項產業也隨之崩潰。由於受薪階級女性暴增，原有的社會秩序也因此顛覆。戰前，這座城市的女性勞動人口極少。然而到了1936年，情況發生了變化，北平有7.6%的女性人口屬於受薪階級。未婚婦女必須負擔的家庭責任較少，往往比已婚婦女更容易找到工作。從事非正式工作的兼職婦女，例如中文家教，人數也有所增加。服務業是當時幫忙撐起中國經濟的行業之一。由於服務業勞工為中國民眾和新來的日本平民提供服務，他們的客群龐大。戰爭爆發後，有兩種職業的女性工作者大幅增加：一種是警察，另一種是打字員。將女性納入警隊的一個主要原因是，只有女警察能夠對其他女性進行搜身。男性罪犯經常利用婦女犯罪，因此讓女警察在公共場所對於女性搜身將有助於減少犯罪。社會對女警察的接受度較高，這也使日本的佔領政權得以執行更嚴密的安全措施。北平女警的主要職責是對婦女和兒童搜身，並且在城門和火車站檢查他們的行李。女警的薪資並不豐厚，只有30日元，約為小學教師的一半，但她們也確實會定期獲得小幅加薪。儘管有些人仍然抵制改變，但也有一些男性認同婦女工作的必要性。某位青島男子寫道，每個人都有義務為社會服務，因此長輩們不應認為出外工作的女性會使家族蒙羞，而應以她們為榮。

新生活運動

　　新生活運動由蔣中正和其妻宋美齡於1934年開始推動，以恢復他們所認為已淪喪的固有道德，並為中國的現代化和戰爭做好準備。蔣中正堅信，中國需要精神力量以擊敗工業化程度更高的日本。他認為，如果中國人能透過軍事化的生活來孕育勇氣，就不需要依賴武器，而日本人也無法摧毀由此而生的精神力量。於是，新生活運動應運而生，以教化和培養民眾成為模範國民，進而賦予中國這股精神力量。為了打好新生活運動的根基，首要任務之一便是教導民眾更好的衛生習慣，並鼓勵養成自律的日常生活。這場運動也試圖透過宣傳來教育國民，藉此弘揚國族主義價值觀，讓人人都能精進自我，而宣傳手段包括改善生活方式的口號與指導方針。例如，鼓勵人們穿著節儉，重慶的男性穿著軍服或西裝，女性則穿著簡單的棉襖。此外，抗戰期間所有茶館都必須張貼國民誓詞等宣傳品。這些誓詞包括誓死不幫助漢奸、誓死不違抗政府、誓死不投降等內容。政府也利用譴責漢奸的名義迫害任何挑戰其權威的人。由於社會大眾往往期待婦女能維持強大的家庭和社會，她們成為這場運動的主要組成。該運動也鼓勵女性穿著樸素端莊，保持整潔，避免浮華。婦女指導委員會等團體則教導婦女如何成為賢妻良母並效忠國家，從而為社會做出貢獻。最後，新生活運動鼓勵將自我精進與更遠大的國家目標相結合。尤其是國家處於戰爭狀態的當下，政府鼓勵國民依照國家需求調整自身作為。儘管這項計劃因為只著重於瑣碎的道德改革，卻忽略了更深層次的體制問題而受到批評，還是在中國史上留下若干不朽的成就。新生活運動強化了自律意識，並傳播儒家價值觀。它協助改善了衛生和傳播公共衛生意識，有助於控制疾病傳播和改善衛生條件。此外，它還透過灌輸國族責任感來動員中國人民參戰。

社會期望的轉變

戰爭期間，傳統就業受到了動搖。戰爭需求挑戰了強調女性做為賢妻良母角色的傳統儒家價值觀。經濟困境和社會規範的轉變使婦女更加投入教育事業。戰時北平的刊物《婦女日報》（Women's Journal）反映出這樣的轉變。雖然其最初鼓勵婦女以家庭內的角色為優先考量，但經濟惡化使此一刊物開始接受婦女投身教育或是其他職場。由於經濟不景氣，許多年輕女性為了找工作和養家而不得不退學。女性經常遭遇性騷擾、工資較低和職場歧視等困境，同時社會還期望她們能養家活口。與美國等諸多西方國家不同的是，中國婦女在戰時取得的成就在戰後依然長期存在。中國共產黨（下稱「中共」）在二戰結束後成為國共內戰的獲勝方，而共產黨對於男女平等和女性工作必要性的主張有助於維持婦女地位。寡婦往往是她們自己和孩子的唯一經濟支柱。隨著高等教育在戰爭期間的擴展，越來越多年輕女性開始在自己的家鄉地區以外工作。由於戰爭對社會規範造成的破壞如此之大，想要在戰後恢復戰前秩序並不可能。

戰火中的兒童

　　想要在戰爭期間留下好的童年回憶，顯然不容易。許多兒童被迫逃離日軍，生活困苦，或是忍受與父母失散的痛苦。對於許多人而言，童年意味著為了生存而不斷遷徙與掙扎。為了養家，兒童經常被迫工作。在難民家庭混亂的逃亡過程中，許多兒童與父母失散，被迫獨自面對恐怖的戰爭。許多家庭不得不行進長達數週或數個月的時間才覓得安全的容身之地。因此，年長的家人還有無法跟上其他家人步伐的兒童有時會被遺棄在路邊等死。許多兒童由於不斷逃難而無法接受適當的教育，甚至連歇息片刻的機會也沒有。居住空間短缺導致不少家庭被迫在衛生條件不佳的窄房裡撫養孩子。據說「亭子間」這種便宜但狹小的起居空間，由於需要額外設置夜壺、板條箱、床舖等家具，擠得就像是倉庫一樣。

　　儘管戰火中的歲月度日如年，但兒童仍然在體育、表演和社群活動中找到了樂趣。傳統遊戲、說書和公共活動讓人們在一片混亂之中獲得了短暫的喘息機會。這些活動也有助於保持文化認同，讓他們逐漸接受戰亂就是生活的常態。戰爭期間，兒童經常與軍隊互動。例如，兒童為部隊表演戲劇，而軍人有時也受命為學校提供軍事訓練，著重於操練和射擊技巧。在某些地區還舉辦了木偶劇和地方戲劇表演來娛樂兒童，並微妙地將愛國主題融入其中，以提高士氣和抵抗佔領軍的意志。

　　二戰期間，美國在珍珠港事件之後於中國駐軍，以協助對抗日軍。這些軍人在不同的情境下遇到了形形色色的中國兒童。他們之間的互動包括提供人道援助還有友誼，以及非正式的教育交流。美國士兵為許多受戰爭影響的兒童提供食物、保護還有情感支持，在這個非常不穩定的時期給予他們些許安定。他們經常分發糖果和口糧給這些兒童，使他們受兒童景仰。在某些情況下，美國軍官與中國地方政府合作，為難民兒童提供援助。美國士兵也教授中國兒童英文單字和西方遊戲,使部分中國兒童學會英文,並模仿美國人的習性舉止。

Santa Claus delights Chinese war orphans at a Christmas party by Saco, China.

在中美特種技術合作所（Sino-American Special Technical Cooperative Organization，簡稱 SACO）舉辦的聖誕派對上，聖誕老人把中國戰爭孤兒逗得露出微笑。

Date of Photo 時間：September 13, 1945
Credits 來源：美國國家檔案館 Photo Courtesy of National Archives

Women do the family washing on the banks of the Pi River.

婦女在沘江水岸上洗滌家中衣物。

Date of Photo 時間：不詳 N/A
Credits 來源：美國國家檔案館 Photo Courtesy of National Archives

A headquarters of the New Life movement located in Hankou, built in a former bank.

新生活運動位於漢口的總部，建築前身為銀行。

Date of Photo 時間：不詳 N/A
Credits 來源：美國國家檔案館 Photo Courtesy of National Archives

Men and children, volunteer workers from nearby villages, work on Burma Road to enable supplies and equipment to get through to front.

男性、兒童與來自鄰近村莊的義工攜手修築滇緬公路,以確保物資和裝備得以運抵前線。

Date of Photo 時間:June 4, 1944
Credits 來源:美國國家檔案館 Photo Courtesy of National Archives

An American army photographer eating his rations with chopsticks under the supervision of a schoolboy.

在身旁中國學童的教導下,一位美國陸軍攝影師用筷子食用口糧。

Date of Photo 時間:May 6, 1944
Credits 來源:美國國家檔案館 Photo Courtesy of National Archives

In Southwest China, children race across rice paddies to greet these US troops with thumbs up signs.

在中國西南部，一群兒童奔越大片稻田，趕來向美國軍人豎起大拇指問好。

Date of Photo 時間：April 25, 1944
Credits 來源：美國國家檔案館 Photo Courtesy of National Archives

Refugees carrying their packs while walking along a railroad line.

一位美軍車隊的騎士載著中國兒童兜風。

Date of Photo 時間：March 2, 1945
Credits 來源：美國國家檔案館 Photo Courtesy of National Archives

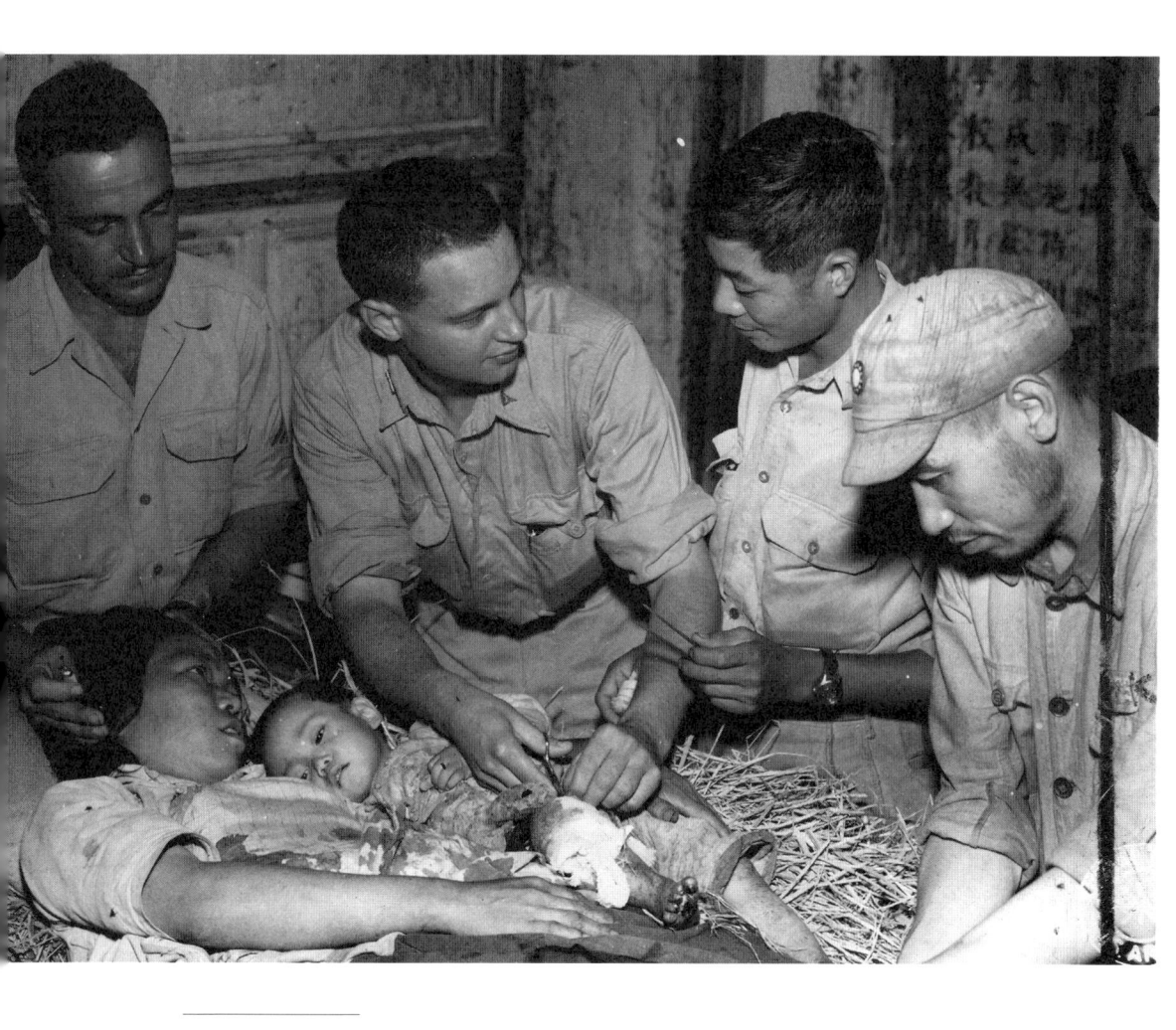

A Chinese woman and her 17-month-old baby are tended to by American medics after being shot by a Japanese sniper.

一位中國母親與她 17 個月大的嬰兒受到日軍狙擊之後，由美國醫護兵悉心照料。

Date of Photo 時間：September 16, 1944
Credits 來源：美國國家檔案館 Photo Courtesy of National Archives

PEASANTS AND
KUNMING

Importance of Kunming and Peasants in Wartime China

The peasant class and the city of Kunming are key to understanding wartime China's socio-political and economic dynamics. From 1937 to 1945, during the Second Sino-Japanese War, the city rose to prominence as a center for military, logistical, and cultural services. Its place as the capital of Yunnan Province and its location far away from the frontlines made it a refuge for many who had to leave their homes because of the war. Kunming became a base for Chinese and American military operations. Furthermore, it served as one of several crucial links in the supply chain for the Allies. Meanwhile, the nation's peasant class continued to face grave dangers, as roughly 80 percent of Chinese people who lived on farms suffered displacement and militarization. Farming life was drastically altered as peasants were conscripted, forced to grow war materiel, or otherwise militarized—and in any case, exploited by corrupt officials seeking to fund the war effort.

This section includes Kunming's transformation into a war zone and the experiences of peasants caught in the currents of war. These two interconnected subjects display the resilience and agency of the most impoverished groups in the country, while shedding light on how regional and rural dynamics shaped the trajectory of the war for modern China.

Kunming as a Wartime Hub

Often regarded as the capital of southwest China, Kunming, during the Second Sino-Japanese War (1937-1945), Kunming was geopolitically important. Although Kunming was far from the actual battlefield, Its geographic location in the rugged terrain of southwestern China made it a critical location. The surrounding mountain chains and difficult terrain protected Kunming, turning it into a natural retreat for the Chinese Nationalist government and an vital location during the war years. It was a buffer against Japanese invasion, and connected China to the Allied forces through the Burma Road and other supply routes. This position was crucial in sustaining the resistance of the Nationalist government and its material support, including military supplies, logistics, and other resources from the Allies.

Kunming also became a haven for displaced populations during the war. This flood of refugees, ranging from high-ranking officials to intellectuals and students,transformed the city into a melting pot of ideas and culture. The intellectuals and artists fleeing the occupied areas carried a treasure trove of cultural and academic resources, further enriching the intellectual landscape in Kunming. At the same time, the city's logistical importance increased by leaps and bounds with the paving of the Burma Road, an overland supply route connecting Kunming with British-controlled Burma, and later due to Allied airlift operations over the "Hump." These supplies provided a flow of supplies into China, allowing the war to continue. In this way, Kunming was logistically indispensable to the war effort.

The pressures of wartime brought about equally dramatic changes in Kunming's infrastructure. The city expanded its roads, warehouses, and transportation networks to serve the needs of the refugees and the war effort. Industries relocated from occupied eastern China and contributed to Kunming's urbanization and industrialization. Not all of this rapid growth was good, though, as tensions between locals and refugees rose as they competed for resources.

Cultural and Educational Contributions

Amid the war, Kunming gradually developed into a cultural and intellectual bulwark. The establishment of the National Southwestern Associated University （西南聯大）, with the three prestigious institutions of Peking University, Tsinghua University, and Nankai University united in their efforts, testified to China's determination to preserve its intellectual traditions. This university became a symbol of resistance, cultivating a spirit of resilience and defiance against Japanese aggression. Kunming's geographical position and relative stability allowed it to serve as a sanctuary for academic pursuits, even amidst wartime chaos. Against all the scarcity of resources and the hardship in living, the faculty and students kept the standard of education high, producing a generation of scholars, scientists, and leaders who would shape China's future.

Kunming also became a center of cultural activity. Scholars, artists, and writers who had fled to the city contributed to a vibrant intellectual and artistic community. Such was the attraction that the likes of Xu Beihong, a painter, and Lao She, a writer, found their refuge in Kunming and carried on with their works from there. The cultural resurgence here helped not only to sustain the rich tradition of Chinese arts and literature, but also in providing a stage for resistance to Japanese aggression. Art and literature produced in Kunming often had themes of resilience and patriotism, adding to the greater war effort by fostering a sense of unity and purpose.

Besides intellectual achievements, Kunming became a center of cultural exchange and grassroots resistance movements. The city held discussions, performances, and exhibitions that showcased the mixture of local and refugee cultures. Meanwhile, Kunming also witnessed the emergence of resistance movements: underground organizations involved in mobilizing resources and people for the war. These movements underlined the duality of the city's role as a bastion of refuge and resistance and how cultural production was linked with political resistance in wartime China.

Challenges Faced by Kunming

Despite its significance as a wartime hub, Kunming still faced numerous challenges that tested its strength. One of the most pressing of these issues was economic hardship. Between the sudden inflow of refugees and the demands of the war effort, local resources became strained, resulting in inflation, food shortages, and increasing unemployment. This led to competition between refugees and city residents for such limited resources, causing social tensions to rise amongst the already poverty-stricken local population. The infrastructure of the city, although expanded, couldn't keep pace with the growing population and economic demands.

Besides, Kunming suffered from the direct impact of Japanese forces, mainly through bombings. These bombings seriously damaged the infrastructure of the city and psychologically traumatized its citizens, a grim and constant reminder that even areas far from the front lines were not safe from the horrors of war. The threat of possible air raids at any moment drove the residents to live in a constant state of vigilance, exacerbating physical and mental health problems.

The social tensions between the refugees and locals became very problematic. These cultural and economic gaps were exacerbated by the presence of educated elites and urbanites in a society that was predominantly rural and agrarian. Refugees usually looked at Kunming as backwards, whereas the local citizens were resentful because the newcomers competed for their scarce resources. Variations in dialect, lifestyle, and social norms significantly hindered integration between the two groups. At the same time, however, the wartime hardships also created some form of solidarity between the two groups as well, given how both contributed to the survival and growth of the city.

Kunming played multiple roles in wartime China: was an important military and logistical hub, it produced many cultural and intellectual contributions, and it faced many challenges as a city under siege. That the city could adapt and thrive under such highly unusual circumstances says much about the resilience of this city and the resourcefulness of its residents. Kunming not only provided valuable resources in China's war but also became a beacon of hope and resistance, leaving a lasting legacy in the nation's history. In its transformations and trials, Kunming epitomized the complexity of wartime China and afforded rich insight into how regional centers shaped the broader trajectory of conflict.

農民與昆明

中國抗戰期間昆明與農民的重要性

　　想了解戰時中國社會政治與經濟動態，農民階級與昆明這座城市都是關鍵所在。1937 年至 1945 年的中國抗日戰爭期間，昆明因為扮演軍事、後勤和文化重鎮的角色而嶄露頭角。遠離前線的昆明是雲南省省會，為許多顛沛流離的人們提供了避難所。昆明成為中美軍事行動的基地。此外，它也是盟軍供應鏈中數個關鍵節點之一。此外，中國的農民階級仍然面臨著嚴重的危險，此時中國有大約 80% 農家人口面臨著流離失所和軍事動員的困境。隨著農民獲徵召入伍、被迫種植戰爭物資，要不然就是接受政府以其他方式進行軍事動員，農民的生活變化可說翻天覆地。無論屬於上述哪一種，他們都受到了尋求戰爭資金的貪官剝削。

　　本章節的內容包括昆明轉變為戰區的過程，以及農民捲入戰爭洪流的經歷。這兩個相互關聯的主題展現了中國最貧困群體的韌性和行動力，同時揭示了地方和鄉村的動態如何形塑現代中國的戰爭軌跡。

作為戰時樞紐的昆明

　　抗日戰爭期間，位於西南地區的昆明是中國的陪都，在地緣政治上舉足輕重。雖然昆明與實際戰場相距甚遠，但其位於中國西南部崎嶇地形的地理位置非常關鍵。周圍的山脈和崎嶇的地形是昆明的天然屏障，使其成為國民政府的撤退根據地和戰爭時期的重要據點。昆明成為抵禦日本侵略的緩衝地帶，並讓中國得以通過滇緬公路和其他補給路線與盟軍部隊聯繫。因為有這樣的地理位置，昆明才得以幫助國民政府維持抵抗作戰以及進行物資後援，而所謂物資包括軍事補給、後勤和其他來自同盟國的資源。

　　在千千萬萬中國人於戰時顛沛流離之際，昆明成為他們的避風港。從高級官員到知識分子和大學生，難民潮將這座城市變成思想和文化的大熔爐。逃離淪陷區的知識份子與藝術家帶著文化與學術資源的寶庫，進一步豐富了昆明的知識格局。與此同時，由於滇緬公路這條連接昆明與英屬緬甸的陸上補給線完工，以及後來盟軍飛越「駝峰」的空運行動，昆明的後勤重要性得到了突飛猛進的提升。這些補給為中國提供了源源不斷的物資，使其得以繼續作戰。昆明對於抗戰的後勤工作而言也因此不可或缺。

戰時壓力同樣為昆明的基礎設施帶來了巨變。這座城市擴建了道路、倉庫和運輸網絡，以滿足難民和戰爭的需求。華東地區遭佔領後工業遷移到昆明，為昆明的都市化和工業化有所貢獻。然而，並非所有的快速增長都是好事；當地人和難民之間的緊張關係隨著雙方爭奪資源而加劇。

文教貢獻

戰爭期間，昆明逐漸發展成為文化與知識的堡壘。北京大學、清華大學、南開大學三所知名學府合併成為國立西南聯合大學（下稱「西南聯大」），充分展現中國保存知識傳統的決心。這所大學成為抵抗日本侵略的象徵，孕育出不屈不撓的反抗精神。昆明的地理位置和相對的穩定，使其即使在戰時的混亂中也能成為學術研究重鎮。在資源匱乏、生活困苦的情況下，師生們仍然保持高水準的教育，培養出一代的學者、科學家和領導人，這些人將形塑中國的未來。

昆明也成為文化活動的中心。逃到這座城市的學者、藝術家和作家打造出一個充滿活力的知識和藝術社群。這樣的吸引力使得畫家徐悲鴻和作家老舍等人以昆明為避風港，得以延續創作生命。這裡的文化復興不僅使豐富的中國藝術和文學傳統得以續命，也為抵抗日本侵略提供了舞臺。在昆明創作的藝術和文學作品往往能展現出堅毅精神，以愛國為主題，透過促進團結和使命感，對抗戰有所貢獻。

除了知識成就以外，昆明也成為文化交流中心和民間抗日運動的重鎮。這座城市舉辦許多討論會、表演和展覽，展示出當地文化與難民文化的交融情形。與此同時，昆明也出現了參與動員資源和民眾投入戰事的地下組織，見證抵抗運動的興起。這些運動突顯出昆明同時扮演避難所和抗戰堡壘的雙重角色，以及戰時中國的文化產出如何與政治抵抗相互聯繫。

昆明所面臨的挑戰

儘管昆明作為戰時的重要樞紐意義非凡，這座城市仍然面臨許多的挑戰，考驗其實力。其中一個最迫切的問題便是經濟困境。由於難民的突然湧入和軍需物資的徵用，當地的資源變得有限，導致通貨膨脹、糧食短缺以及失業率上升。這也造成難民與當地居民之間對有限資源展開競爭，使本已貧困的當地居民之間的社會關係更加緊張。這座城市的基礎建設雖然有所擴建，但仍無法跟上人口與經濟需求的增長。

此外，昆明還受到日軍的空襲、轟炸等軍事行動直接影響。這些轟炸嚴重破壞了城市的基礎設施，也為市民帶來了心理創傷，不斷無情地提醒人們即使是遠離前線的地區也無法避免戰爭的恐怖。隨時可能遭受空襲的威脅使居民在日常生活中仍然時時保持警戒，也使身心健康問題惡化。

難民與當地人之間的社會矛盾變得非常棘手。在一個原本以農業為主的農村社會裡，受過教育的精英和都市人的出現，更加劇了這樣的文化和經濟差距。難民通常將昆明視為落後的地方，而當地居民則因為新住民爭奪他們稀缺的資源而感到不滿。方言、生活方式和社會規範的不同也明顯阻礙了兩個群體之間的融合。然而，與此同時，因為兩個群體都為這座城市的生存與發展做出了貢獻，戰時的艱辛也使雙方在某種形式上團結了起來。

昆明在戰時中國扮演了多重角色：它是重要的軍事與後勤樞紐，在文化與知識方面貢獻良多，作為一個被圍困的城市也面對了許多挑戰。在極度不尋常的環境中，昆明卻能夠適應並蓬勃發展，很大程度上說明了它是個堅忍不拔的城市，居民則是善於應變與適應。昆明不僅為中國的抗戰提供了寶貴的資源，而且還成為了希望與抵抗的燈塔，在中國史上留下不可磨滅的印記。昆明在轉變與試煉之中體現戰時中國的複雜性，也讓我們得以洞察地方上的多重中心如何形塑出範圍更廣的戰爭軌跡。

Jan 30th, 1945 in Kunming, China. Jeannette is taken to school on a bike by her brother, Bob. While her sister Margie, mummy and dad are waving good-bye.

1945年1月30日攝於中國昆明。珍妮特的哥哥鮑伯騎著腳踏車載她上學,她的姐妹瑪姬與父母則為他們揮手送行。

Date of Photo 時間：January 30, 1945
Credits 來源：美國國家檔案館 Photo Courtesy of National Archives

Mar 31, 1945 in Kunming, China. A burial ceremony officiated by Chaplain George Moeller, Duluth, Minn for LT. Daniel B Martin, Webster Grove, MO., and Maj. Carlton Dutton.

1945 年 3 月 31 日攝於中國昆明。丹尼爾・B・馬丁中尉（來自密蘇里州韋伯斯特格羅夫市）與卡爾頓・達頓少校的葬禮，由部隊牧師喬治・莫勒（來自明尼蘇達州杜魯斯市）主持。

Date of Photo 時間：March 31, 1945
Credits 來源：美國國家檔案館 Photo Courtesy of National Archives

March 24th, 1945 at the Youth Army headquarters in Kunming, China. An inspection tour that consists of (from left to right), Lt. Gen. Liang Hwa Shum, Lt. Gen. Tu In Ming, Generalissimo Chiang Kai-Shek, Gen. Wei Lih Waung, Gen. Fang Shen Chueh.

1945年3月24日攝於中國昆明的青年軍總部。視察團（左起）由梁華盛中將、杜聿明中將、蔣中正特級上將、衛立煌上將、方先覺上將等人組成。

Date of Photo 時間：March 24, 1945
Credits 來源：美國國家檔案館 Photo Courtesy of National Archives

June 4th, 1945. In the east of Kunming, China. U.S. Army road engineers who helped build the Stilwell Road are now working to improve highways. The engineers overcame difficult terrain to construct the road in the image, which was critical in breaking the land blockade of China. In the image, the U.S. engineers are collaborating with Chinese officials to upgrade the roads for better transport.

1945 年 6 月 4 日攝於中國昆明東方山谷。協助修築史迪威公路（Stilwell Road）的美軍道路工程師正著手改善高速公路。他們必須克服艱難的地形以修築圖中的道路。當時中國的陸路交通遭日軍封鎖，這條道路對於突破封鎖能發揮關鍵作用。圖中，美國工程師正與中國官員合作提升道路品質以改善交通。

Date of Photo 時間：June 4, 1945
Credits 來源：美國國家檔案館 Photo Courtesy of National Archives

Burma Road through China hills between Kunming and Kweiyang, China.

昆明至貴陽段的滇緬公路穿越中國境內的重巒疊嶂。

Date of Photo 時間：ca. 1941-1942
Credits 來源：美國國家檔案館 Photo Courtesy of National Archives

The crowds in the streets await Ching Pi Loo upon its arrival in Kunming during a convoy roll.

昆明金碧路上的人群正翹首期盼車隊的到來。

Date of Photo 時間：ca. 1942
Credits 來源：美國國家檔案館 Photo Courtesy of National Archives

THE WARTIME EXPERIENCE OF PEASANTS

Economic Impact on Peasants

The Second Sino-Japanese War deeply disrupted the lives of China's peasant majority, changing their daily lives and propelling them into general destitution. One of the most immediate effects was the requisition of land and property. Both the advancing Japanese army and the retreating Nationalist forces often seized farmland to support military operations, leaving peasants dispossessed and without means of subsistence. Entire villages were destroyed, forcing families to abandon their homes and livelihoods.

Apart from land loss, the peasants also had to carry the burden of increased taxation and obligatory labor imposed by the Nationalist and Communist armies to sustain the war efforts. Many peasants had to give out grain, livestock, and other supplies, which usually left them with barely enough to make ends meet. Labor conscription for infrastructural projects, such as road and fortification building, depleted resources and time, and disrupted agricultural production.

Agriculture and food supplies were also severely disrupted, as so much of the countryside was occupied or laid waste to in battles. Military forces destroyed or seized crops, causing widespread famine. Inaccessibility to markets amidst war-induced chaos made it impossible for many rural families even to exchange goods for necessities. Just as history has shown, the peasants once again bore the greatest brunt of the war's material costs.

Peasants and the Resistance Effort

Despite these difficulties, peasants played a very important role in China's resistance to Japanese occupation, becoming the backbone of resistance groups in most areas. They waged guerrilla warfare, drawing on their knowledge of the local terrain. Peasant guerrilla fighters would sabotage, ambush, and gather intelligence to effectively disrupt the supply lines and communication networks of the Japanese. Such acts of defiance demonstrated the resolute will to resist among peasants faced with overwhelming odds.

Another important ingredient of resistance was the formation of peasant militias by Communist and Nationalist forces. Of the two, the Communists were particularly adept at organizing the countryside to create a foundation for their long-term strategy of engaging the Japanese while solidifying their support among the peasantry. These militia groups were provided much-needed manpower and logistical support, often at great personal risk. However, there wasn't complete harmony in collaboration between peasants and organized resistance forces. The conflicting agendas of the Nationalist and Communist forces sometimes placed contradictory demands on peasant communities, straining their limited resources and creating divisions within rural society.

The peasant involvement in the resistance underlined their agency and determination for the defense of their homes and communities. Often portrayed as victims, many peasants chose to resist, a fact that outlined their critical role in shaping the war effort.

Social and Cultural Changes

The war brought significant social and cultural changes to rural China, altering the lives of peasants in fundamental ways. One of the most visible impacts of the war was wartime migration, where millions of rural residents fled their villages to escape Japanese occupation or conscription by Chinese forces. This migration disrupted traditional community structures but also exposed peasants to new ideas, ideologies, and ways of life. The movement of soldiers, intellectuals, and refugees across the countryside spread revolutionary ideas and nationalist sentiments that would provide the backdrop to future social and political change.

One of the biggest changes was the increase in literacy campaigns and political awareness. Most noticeably, the Communist Party had initiated programs of education within the areas it controlled to teach peasants reading and writing as broader aspects of their political mobilization. These campaigns created a sense of empowerment for the peasants and helped them to identify more and more with revolutionary ideologies. The company of soldiers and intellectuals further widened their horizons regarding national and global issues, dismantling the conventional beliefs and implanting a feeling of closeness with the broader struggles of the Chinese nation.

The war further catalyzed changes in gender roles among rural communities: with many men conscripted or killed, women increasingly took over responsibilities traditionally reserved for men, including farming, decision making, and even participation in resistance activities. For many, this shift foreshadowed possibilities of greater equality between the genders in the years to come.

Hardships and Suffering

But of all, peasants suffered the most because of the war consequences: the life of peasants was so heavily afflicted during the time. Among other things, the Japanese followed an infamous policy known as the "Three Alls Policy" (kill all, burn all, loot all). The villagers were massacred, women raped, and houses deliberately razed to ground. These atrocities have created a deep impact on the collective memory of rural communities, instilling in them hate against the Japanese occupation and the determination to resist.

Another heavy burden was displacement: millions of peasants were forced to flee their houses and joined the refugees living in unsanitary conditions of overcrowding. Such families suffered hunger, exposure to weather, and a day-to-day fight to get hold of even the most basic essentials of living. For those who remained within the occupied territories, life was just as bad: obligatory labor, extortions, and surveillance by Japanese forces were routine events.

Health crises furthered the suffering of rural populations. Epidemics of cholera, typhoid, and malaria spread rapidly in unsanitary conditions, both in refugee camps and war-torn villages. With minimal access to medical care and a lack of resources to combat these outbreaks, many rural families suffered devastating losses. Malnutrition and starvation weakened immune systems, further weakening the peasantry against illness.

It is quite astonishing, however, to see how China's peasants faced up to all these hardships. The readiness with which they adapted to altered circumstances, resisted, and contributed to the war effort underlined their importance in shaping the course of the conflict. As much as they suffered greatly, the peasants' wartime experiences also sowed seeds that prepared the social and political transformations that would take place in the postwar era.

The wartime experiences of the peasant class of China reflect, in all possible ways, the huge impact of the Second Sino-Japanese War on rural society: from economic devastation and forced migration to active participation in resistance efforts, peasants were at once victims and agents of change. The war brought immense suffering but also fostered new social and cultural dynamics which would shape the future of China. By examining the peasants' lives during this turbulent period, we gain a deeper understanding of the many complexities of wartime China and its resilient rural population.

Wartime experiences between Kunming City and the countryside contrasted so dramatically. Being a wartime hub, Kunming experienced rapid urbanization with huge inflows of refugees, intellectuals, and high-ranking officials. The infrastructure here was extended toward military logistics, education, and cultural activities. On the minus side, the transformation brought on resource strain, economic inflation, and social tensions between natives and refugees. On the other hand, rural districts were reduced to smithereens: destroyed villages, requisitioned farmlands, uprooted communities, and peasants had to bear the brunt of economic exploitation through increased taxations, forced labor, and disruption in agricultural cycles because of which peasants suffered poverty and famine across many regions.

Despite such discontinuities, Kunming and the countryside were inextricably linked. The countryside supplied Kunming with crucial necessities like grain, livestock, and labor, feeding the city's burgeoning wartime economy as well as its refugee population. In turn, Kunming was a center of resistance organization, funnelling resources back to the countryside in the forms of guerrilla warfare and peasant militias. The city was also a cultural and intellectual beacon: refugees fleeing the city, soldiers, or educators carried political awareness and the novel ideologies to the countryside.

In all these ways, the interdependence of Kunming with the countryside brings into sharp focus the complexity of wartime China. As much as the countryside suffered more, their contribution to maintaining Kunming as a hub city during wartime was important. In turn, the political, logistic, and cultural work of Kunming increased the intensity of rural resistance, making their experiences interdependent during wartime. This complex interaction influenced the wider war effort and postwar transformation of Chinese society.

Political Impacts

The wartime ordeals of Kunming and the countryside played a very important role in the political reshaping of China, especially in the rise of the Communist Party of China. The war greatly helped the Communist Party of China to increase its support base by mobilizing peasants. Organizing guerrilla resistance and appealing to peasant grievances, such as land redistribution and fair treatment, the CCP built up a legitimate and attractive reputation among the peasantry. This was in line with the peasants' interests and contrasted sharply with the Nationalist government's reliance on forced requisitions and taxation that alienated much of the rural population.

Kunming's wartime role also influenced post-war politics. As an intellectual and cultural center of resistance, the city became a place of discourse on China's future and critiques of Nationalist policies. The intellectual movements in Kunming gave ideological underpinning to political change, encouraging a vision of modernization and reform. Besides, wartime collaboration between rural resistance fighters and urban planners created a foundation for post-war political consolidation that helped the CCP win power.

Social and Cultural Legacy

The wartime experiences in Kunming and rural China created a social and cultural legacy that was profound. Intellectual movements during the war, epitomized by such institutions as National Southwestern Associated University, left their imprint on Chinese culture. Ideas nurtured in Kunming, like nationalism, resistance, and reform, echoed well beyond the war. Many of the Kunming residents then were intellectuals and students who later on became leading figures in academia, politics, and society, shaping the cultural and intellectual trajectory of modern China.

The war started a tidal wave of major social changes in the rural areas. The wartime hardships disturbed the traditional structures and allowed the easy penetration of new ideas on literacy, political consciousness, and strength through organization. The CCP took advantage of these changes to prematurely proclaim land reforms and mobilize the countryside in favor of its post-war program. The war also reconstituted the role of gender in rural settings, as women took on new responsibilities and leadership roles during the conflict that challenged traditional patriarchal norms.

Economic Recovery and Reconstruction

In this way, the wartime experiences of Kunming and the countryside informed their post-war economic recovery. Having greatly expanded its infrastructure and industrial capacity during the war, Kunming became a regional economic center in southwest China. Since hostilities were over, resources could be diverted from military to civilian uses, facilitating urban growth and modernization. Cultural and intellectual legacies of Kunming's wartime population further contributed toward its growth into an educational and administrative hub.

The rural areas had to recover much more difficultly, considering how much farmland, infrastructure, and communities were destroyed. On the contrary, war catalyzed changes which influenced reconstruction. Wartime collectivization and mobilization strategies pursued by the Communist Party of China provided a background for post-war rural reforms in the redistribution of land and agricultural modernization. The transition from a wartime to peacetime economy was supposed to rebuild agricultural productivity along with inequalities that have driven peasant discontent during the war.

The wartime experiences of Kunming and rural China had wide-ranging implications for the nation's political, social, and economic development. It was the struggles and transformations of this period that propelled the CCP to power, reshaped rural society, and created Kunming as a cultural and economic center. These changes together underpinned modern China and testify to the continuing power of wartime resistance and resilience. The interaction of urban and rural dynamics during the war underlines the interdependency of China's transformation, of how local experiences contributed to the shaping of the course of national history.

Kunming and China's peasants were important components that made up the modern narrative of wartime China. Kunming, during this period as a wartime hub, emerged as a haven for intellectuals, refugees, and government operations; its strategic location allowed for vital supply routes such as the Burma Road. The cultural and intellectual contributions of the city represented resilience, whereby institutions like the National Southwestern Associated University nurtured ideas that would shape China's post-war development. Meanwhile, the rural peasantry bore the brunt of economic exploitation, displacement, and violence but demonstrated remarkable resilience and agency by actively participating in guerrilla resistance and supporting the broader war effort.

The interrelation between urban Kunming and the countryside speaks to the many layers of China's experience during wartime. The countryside furnished important resources and labor for Kunming's wartime economy and its resistance, while the city became a center of organizing support and spreading revolutionary ideas in the countryside. It is shared struggles that gave a sense of cohesion across geographical and social boundaries.

The wartime challenges faced by Kunming and rural China brought out the resilience of their citizens and created ground for political, social, and economic changes that defined modern China and set the stage for its post-war reconstruction and progress.

農民的
戰時經歷

對農民的經濟影響

　　農民階層在中國社會人口中比例最高，對日抗戰讓他們的生活天翻地覆，不但日常生活變調，還普遍陷入貧困。其中最直接的影響是土地和財產的徵用。無論是進攻的日軍還是撤退的國軍，都經常搶奪農田以支援軍事行動，導致農民被剝奪財產，頓失維生之道。許多村莊遭徹底摧毀，迫使家庭放棄他們的家園和生計。

　　除了土地方面的損失之外，農民還必須承擔國軍和共軍為了繼續作戰而強加的稅收和強制勞動的負擔。許多農民不得不上繳穀物、牲畜和其他物資，這使他們通常僅能勉強糊口。道路和防禦工事等基建工程的勞力徵募耗盡資源和時間，並干擾了農業生產。

　　由於農村大部分遭佔領或是在戰火中被徹底蹂躪，農業和糧食供應也受到了嚴重破壞。軍隊摧毀或搶劫農作物，造成大規模的飢荒。由於市場在戰爭引發的混亂中無法運作，使得許多農村家庭甚至無法透過以物易物來換取生活必需品。跟過去的歷史一樣，農民再次承受戰爭中物資損失的最大衝擊。

農民與抗日運動

　　儘管面臨這些困難，農民在抵抗日軍佔領的行動中扮演了非常重要的角色，成為大多數地區抗日組織的骨幹。他們利用自己對於當地地形的瞭解發動游擊戰。農民游擊隊員會進行破壞活動、伏擊日軍並收集情報，以有效破壞日軍的補給線和通訊網絡。這些反抗行動展現出農民即使面臨絕境也能維持堅定的抵抗意志。

　　抗日作戰的另一個要素是共軍和國軍組成的農民民兵。在這兩者之中，共產黨尤其擅長把農村地區居民組織起來，為他們與日本人戰鬥的長期戰略奠定基礎，同時鞏固他們在農民當中的支持度。他們往往冒著巨大的個人風險，為這些民兵團體提供急需的人力和後勤支援。然而，農民與抗日組織之間的合作並非完全和諧。國民黨和共產黨勢力的意圖不一，有時會對農民社群提出相互矛盾的要求，使他們有限的資源捉襟見肘，並在農村社會中造成分歧。

農民參與抵抗活動，突顯了他們保衛家園和社群的行動力和決心。許多農民經常被描繪成受害者，但他們卻選擇了抵抗，而這也展現出他們在支援抗戰當中的關鍵作用。

社會與文化變革

這場戰爭為中國農村帶來了重大的社會和文化變革，從根本上改變了農民的生活。戰時移民是抗戰最明顯的影響之一，就是千千萬萬農村居民逃離他們的村莊，只為避開日本佔領或中國軍隊的徵兵。這種遷徙破壞了傳統的社群結構，但也使農民接觸到新的思想、意識形態與生活方式。士兵、知識分子和難民在鄉間流動，散播了革命思想和國族主義情緒，進而隱約影響了未來的社會和政治變革。

最大的變化之一是「掃盲運動」的開展和政治意識的提升。最明顯的是，此一運動是中共更廣泛政治動員的一環，他們在控制區內發起了教育計劃，教導農民讀書寫字。這些運動為農民創造了一種賦權感，並讓他們愈來愈認同革命的意識形態。伴隨著他們的士兵和知識分子進一步拓展他們對國家和全球問題的視野，瓦解傳統觀念，深深感到自己與整體中華民族休戚與共，為救亡圖存而鬥爭。

戰爭進一步催化了農村社區中性別角色的轉變：隨著許多男性奉召入伍或遇害，婦女逐漸接手傳統上歸為男性的責任，包括耕作、參與決策，甚至加入抗日活動。對許多人而言，這樣的轉變預示著在未來的歲月中，兩性之間可能會更為平等。

困境與受苦

但在所有人當中，農民所受的戰爭禍害最深：農民的生活在那段時期受到極其嚴重的影響。尤其是日軍奉行惡名昭彰的所謂「三光政策」：

殺光、燒光、搶光。他們屠殺村民，強姦婦女，蓄意將屋舍夷為平地。這些暴行對鄉村社區的集體記憶產生了深遠的影響，讓他們不僅對日本佔領軍懷恨在心，也更加堅決抵抗。

另一個沉重的負擔是被迫遷徙：數百萬農民不得不逃離家園，與其他難民一同生活在人滿為患、不衛生的環境中。這些家庭飽受飢餓、風霜雨雪之苦，每天都為謀取基本的生活必需品而奮鬥。對於那些留在佔領區的人而言，生活同樣難堪，強制勞動、強取豪奪和日軍監視都是日常生活中不可避免的。

健康危機加深了農村人口的痛苦。在難民營和飽受戰爭踐躪的村莊等不衛生的環境下，霍亂、傷寒和瘧疾等流行病迅速蔓延。由於獲得醫療照護的機會極少，而且缺乏資源來對抗疫情，許多農村家庭因此遭受了毀滅性的損失。營養不良和飢餓削弱了免疫系統，進一步削弱了農民對疾病的抵抗力。

然而，中國農民面對此等困境的表現實在令人歎為觀止。他們隨時準備適應變動的環境，抵抗並為抗戰做出貢獻，突顯了他們在形塑戰爭進程中的重要性。儘管農民遭受了巨大的苦難，但他們的戰時經歷也播下了種子，為戰後的社會和政治變革做好了準備。

中國農民階級的戰時經歷從各方面反映了中國抗日戰爭對農村社會的巨大影響：從經濟破壞、被迫遷徙到積極參與抗戰，農民既是受害者，也是變革的推動者。這場戰爭帶來了巨大的苦難，但也孕育了新的社會和文化動力，這樣的動力即將塑造中國的未來。我們可以透過檢視農民在這段動盪時期的生活更加深入了解戰時中國的錯綜複雜，以及農村人口的堅毅不撓。

昆明市與農村在戰時的經歷形成了強烈的對比。昆明作為戰時樞紐，隨著大量難民、知識分子和高官的湧入而經歷了快速的都市化。這裡的基礎建設開始延伸到軍事後勤、教育和文化活動等方面。不利的一面是，這樣的轉型也帶來了資源緊繃、經濟通膨，以及當地人與難民之間社會局勢緊張等問題。另一方面，農村地區的慘狀令人不忍卒睹：村莊被摧毀、農田遭徵收、全村居民不得不遠走他方。農民承受經濟剝削的重擔，包括增加稅收、強迫勞動、農業生產週期中斷，許多地區的農民因此遭受貧困和饑荒。

儘管昆明與農村的情況有著天壤之別，兩地之間仍有著千絲萬縷的關係。農村為昆明提供了穀物、牲畜和勞動力等重要必需品，為該市蓬勃發展的戰時經濟和難民人口輸入必要資源。反而言之，昆明則是抵抗組織的中心，將資源注入農村，用以援助游擊隊和農民民兵。這座城市也是文化與知識的燈塔，逃離該地的難民、士兵或是教育家將政治意識與新穎的意識形態帶進了農村。

透過這些層面，昆明與農村的相互依存關係使得戰時中國的複雜性成為矚目焦點。儘管農村遭受更多的苦難，但他們對於維持昆明作為戰時樞紐城市的貢獻非常重要。反過來說，昆明的政治、後勤和文化工作增強了農村的抵抗，使他們的戰時經歷相互依存。這種複雜的互動影響了更廣泛的抗戰行動以及戰後中國社會的轉變。

政治影響

戰時昆明和農村的磨難對中國的政治版圖的重塑，尤其是中共的崛起，發揮了非常重要的作用。這場戰爭大大幫助了中共透過動員農民來擴充其民意基礎。中共組織了游擊隊來抵抗，並訴諸於土地重新分配、公平待遇等改變以吸引對現狀不滿的農民，讓農民在心中對中共具有正當性與吸引力的印象。這符合農民的利益，與此形成強烈對比的是國民政府主要以農村地區為強制徵收和徵稅的對象，讓大部分的農村居民對政府離心離德。

昆明的戰時角色也影響了戰後政治。作為抗戰期間的知識和文化中心，這座城市成為了討論中國的未來和批判國民政府政策的地方。昆明的思想運動為政治變革提供意識形態基礎，促進現代化和改革的願景。此外，戰時農村抗日鬥士與城市規劃者之間的合作為戰後政治局勢的鞏固奠定了基礎，幫助中共贏得了政權。

社會與文化遺產

　　昆明與中國農村的戰時經驗在社會與文化方面影響深遠。抗戰期間，以西南聯大等機構為代表的知識份子運動在中國文化中留下了烙印。在昆明孕育的思想，如民族主義、抵抗和改革精神，在戰後仍迴響不止。當時許多昆明居民都是知識分子和學生，後來他們成為學術、政治和社會等領域的領導人物，塑造了現代中國的文化和學術走向。

　　戰爭在農村地區引發了重大社會變革的浪潮。戰時人民的艱困處境擾亂了傳統架構，使得關於文化、政治意識和組織力量的新思想得以輕易滲透。中共利用這些變化極早宣佈土地改革，並動員農村支持其戰後計畫。這場戰爭還重塑了農村環境中的性別角色，因為婦女在戰爭中承擔了新的責任與領導角色，對傳統父權規範構成挑戰。

經濟復甦與重建

　　如此一來，昆明和農村的戰時經歷為戰後經濟復甦提供了參考。昆明在戰爭期間大幅擴展了基礎建設和工業能力，成為中國西南地區的經濟中心。既然戰爭已經結束，資源便可以由軍事轉移至民生用途，促進城市的發展與現代化。昆明戰時人口留下的文化和知識遺產使其進一步發展為教育和行政中心。

　　考量到耕地、基礎設施和社群被摧毀的程度，農村地區的恢復勢必困難得多。相反的，戰爭促成了變化，並進一步影響重建。中共在戰時推行的集體化和動員策略，成為了戰後土地重新分配和農業現代化等方面農村改革的先聲。從戰爭到和平時期的經濟過渡理應重建農業生產力，並消除戰時導致農民不滿的不平等現象。

　　昆明和中國農村的戰時經歷對於國家的政治、社會和經濟發展產生了規模龐大的影響。正是這段時期的鬥爭和轉型，將中共推往權力巔峰，重塑農村社會，並將昆明打造成文化和經濟中心。這些變化共同撐起現代中國，並證明戰時抵抗和堅毅的力量川流不息。戰爭期間城市和農村的動態互動突顯出中國轉型期間兩者相互依存的情形,以及地方上的經驗如何參與塑造國家的歷史進程。

在現代關於抗戰時期中國的敘事裡,昆明與中國農民皆是其重要組成部分。在這段時期,昆明作為戰時樞紐,成為知識份子、難民與政府運作的避風港;其戰略位置使得滇緬公路等重要補給路線得以開通。這座城市的文化和知識貢獻代表了其韌性,而諸如西南聯大這樣的機構則孕育了即將塑造中國戰後發展的思想。與此同時,農村的農民首當其衝地受到經濟剝削、強制遷徙和暴力對待,但他們透過積極參與游擊抵抗和為了抗戰提供支援,展現出非凡的韌性和行動力。

昆明這座城市與農村之間的相互關係足以展現出中國戰時經驗的層次有多豐富。農村為昆明的戰時經濟和抗戰提供了重要的資源和勞動力,而城市則成為農村籌劃支援和傳播革命思想的中心。正是兩地共同的奮鬥,使得彼此跨越了地域和社會的界限,產生了凝聚力。

昆明和中國農村在戰時面臨的挑戰突顯了公民的韌性,為規劃現代中國的政治、社會和經濟變革建立了根據,並為其戰後的重建和進展奠定了基礎。

Chinese peasant farmers irrigate their rice fields with paddles using their feet.

中國農民用腳踩水車以灌溉稻田。

Date of Photo 時間：ca. 1930
Credits 來源：美國國家檔案館 Photo Courtesy of National Archives

Chinese farmers are paddling water into rice paddles by foot. The food is later used to feed American Airmen flying against Japan from bases in Western China.

中國農民用腳踩水車,將水打入稻田。這些糧食之後將供應給在中國西部與日軍作戰的美軍飛行員。

Date of Photo 時間:ca. 1943
Credits 來源:美國國家檔案館 Photo Courtesy of National Archives

The rice field of farmer Chen, Chen uses the water buffalo to pull the plow that prepares the rice field.

農夫老陳的稻田，水牛正在幫他犁田。

Date of Photo 時間：ca. 1944
Credits 來源：美國國家檔案館 Photo Courtesy of National Archives

Farmer Wang Hung and Ching both using the two water buffalos to pull the plow that prepares the rice field.

兩頭水牛正在幫農夫王泓（音譯）與王清（音譯）拉犁耕田。

Date of Photo 時間：ca. 1945
Credits 來源：美國國家檔案館 Photo Courtesy of National Archives

A farmer and his wife in the dry uplands of Kansa province, Northwest China, weeding their crops by hand.
農民夫婦在乾燥的中國西北部甘肅省高地徒手除草。

Date of Photo 時間：ca. 1945
Credits 來源：美國國家檔案館 Photo Courtesy of National Archives

Chinese farmers digging rice shoots from a seed bed. The food is later used to supply for the American airmen based in the Western part of China.

中國農民從苗床掘出稻穗。這些糧食之後將供應給駐紮在中國西部的美軍飛行員。

Date of Photo 時間：ca. 1944
Credits 來源：美國國家檔案館 Photo Courtesy of National Archives

A mom and her daughter are gathering soy bean harvests in Szechuan Province, China.

中國四川省一對母女正在整理採收而來的大豆。

Date of Photo 時間：ca. 1945
Credits 來源：美國國家檔案館 Photo Courtesy of National Archives

A Chinese farmer uses 5 horses to farm.

五匹馬正在幫中國農夫耕田。

Date of Photo 時間：ca. 1930-40
Credits 來源：美國國家檔案館 Photo Courtesy of National Archives

Chinese farmers use horses to plant soybeans.

馬匹幫助中國農夫種植大豆。

Date of Photo 時間：ca. 1930-40
Credits 來源：美國國家檔案館 Photo Courtesy of National Archives

Farmers are on their way to the streets of Pishan to sell their products on market day.

一群趕集的農夫,他們正要前往皮山縣市區去銷售農產品。

Date of Photo 時間:ca. 1940
Credits 來源:美國國家檔案館 Photo Courtesy of National Archives

Farmers are on their way to the streets of Pishan to sell their products at the market.

農夫們為了趕集銷售他們的農產,正在往皮山縣的路上。

Date of Photo 時間:ca. 1942
Credits 來源:美國國家檔案館 Photo Courtesy of National Archives

A sturdy Chinese woman farmer carrying a load of hay with a bamboo on her shoulder.

健壯的中國農女用竹竿將稻草挑在肩上。

Date of Photo 時間：ca. 1943
Credits 來源：美國國家檔案館 Photo Courtesy of National Archives

A Chinese village.

中國農村。

Date of Photo 時間：ca. 1944
Credits 來源：美國國家檔案館 Photo Courtesy of National Archives

PEOPLE

The Hump Airlift began in 1942 after Japan cut off China's supply routes by occupying Burma. The U.S. Army Air Force flew vital supplies over the Himalayan Mountains from India to China, helping China continue its fight against Japan. The Chinese people played a crucial role by building airstrips, providing ground support, and assisting with logistics. Later, Chinese pilots teamed up with American pilots in a joint effort known as the China-US Air Force Mixed Formation. This airlift was essential in maintaining Allied support in the Pacific during World War II.

Chinese and American Cooperation During the Hump Airlift

During the Hump Airlift, the cooperation between the Chinese people and the U.S. army went beyond logistics and security, extending into shared meals and daily interactions. Chinese laborers, often called "coolies," played a vital role by constructing runways and support structures in the challenging, high-altitude terrain. With limited tools and harsh conditions, they cleared land, leveled surfaces, and built essential facilities like storage and fuel depots. As American pilots flew over the treacherous Himalayas, transporting crucial supplies to China, they depended on Chinese support at the airstrips to unload and prepare supplies. The partnership between the two groups was forged not only in the practicalities of war but in the simple, everyday act of eating and working together.

American soldiers and Chinese workers often shared meals, fostering camaraderie amid the war's hardships. While U.S. rations were provided, they were sometimes insufficient for the harsh mountain conditions. The Chinese locals, accustomed to traditional foods, would share their rice, vegetables, and occasionally meat to help feed the soldiers. The food was sometimes prepared miles away and delivered to the troops on their long and grueling journeys. They ate the shared meals wherever possible—on the road or at makeshift rest stops. These shared meals helped bridge cultural gaps, with language barriers softened through cooperation and mutual support.

Surviving Through Skills

Even amid the chaos of war, the marketplaces in China remained bustling hubs of life and energy. As traditional livelihoods were disrupted during the war, small businesses became essential for survival. In crowded marketplaces, women sold handmade scarves, which not only served as practical items but also showcased local craftsmanship and resilience. Farmers gathered fruits and nuts, which grew naturally in the region, and sold them to make ends meet, which became a crucial source of nutrition during food shortages in the war.

The market was more than just a place for trade—it was a symbol of perseverance. Despite the war, street corners and open spaces were alive with the sounds of martial artists and acrobats, who performed their ancient skills to earn a living. These acts, deeply rooted in Chinese tradition, brought brief moments of wonder and joy to war-weary people. For the performers, performing and traveling from town to town was not only a way to survive but a means of keeping their culture alive.

With families torn apart by the war, letter writers became essential in keeping people connected, composing messages for those who couldn't write or read. At the same time, fortune-telling, a deep-rooted tradition, offered comfort and direction in times of uncertainty. These services were in high demand in the market, providing a way for educated Chinese who had lost their jobs to support their families, while also offering hope and guidance to those navigating the darkness of war.

As many men were away fighting, women took on jobs in factories, farming, and selling goods in local markets. They managed households, cared for children, and made clothing to sell. Children assisted with factory work, gathering firewood, and even working in the fields and factories. Despite the hardships, these women and children demonstrated incredible resilience, helping their families endure the challenges of wartime life.

Helping the Impoverished and Orphans

As cities were destroyed, families torn apart, and the economy collapsed, beggars became a common sight in China. Women, children, and the elderly gathered in markets or on street corners, hoping for food or money. With resources scarce and families scattered, begging became one of the few ways to survive. The large number of beggars reflected the widespread hardship caused by the war.

To address this growing problem, the Salvation Army, along with other organizations, set up a camp for beggars. The camp could house up to 2,000 people at a time and provided vital support to those left starving and homeless. With police assistance, beggars were rounded up and taken off the streets of the International Settlement. Inside the camp, they were given food, clothing, and shelter in bamboo huts. The camp also offered a school, a gospel house, and a workshop, giving people a chance to rebuild their lives and regain their dignity.

Meanwhile, orphanages became essential for children who had lost their parents during the war. Charitable organizations provided shelter, food, and safety for these children, giving them hope and a sense of stability amid the chaos. Orphanages also offered education, ensuring that despite the trauma they had endured, these children had opportunities to learn and grow. For many, orphanages were the only place where they could begin to heal and regain a sense of normalcy during wartime.

Trends in Chinese Fashion

During the Second World War, China's fashion began to change as the country faced Japanese invasions and internal struggles. Traditional garments like the *Changpao* (a long robe), *Magua* (a short jacket with loose trousers for men), and *Qipao* (a form-fitting dress for women) remained common, but wartime conditions prompted a shift. The Chinese Tunic Suit (or *Sun Yat-sen suit*) became popular as a symbol of unity and resilience, with its simple, practical design meeting the needs of the time. Western-style suits also gained popularity among the urban elite, seen as symbols of modernity and sophistication. Changes in hats and shoes followed suit. Men replaced traditional Futou hats with the more functional Sun Yat-sen hat, complementing the military-inspired Tunic Suit, while women opted for simpler, practical head coverings. Footwear also became more durable, with men favoring military-style boots and women choosing comfortable, practical shoes. These changes in clothing, hats, and shoes reflected China's attempt to balance tradition with the demands of a modern, wartime world.

Hairstyles also changed as part of this broader shift. Traditionally, men wore long hair or topknots, while women styled their hair in elaborate updos or braids. But as the war progressed, especially in cities, more practical and simplified styles emerged. Men started adopting shorter, cleaner cuts, which were easier to maintain and suited the military-inspired Tunic Suit. Women, too, moved away from complex hairstyles, opting for simpler, shorter cuts or waves that were more practical given the wartime conditions. These changes in both clothing and hairstyles were part of China's attempt to modernize while staying grounded in its cultural roots during a time of uncertainty.

Transformation of Chinese Culture

A divide also emerged between the older and younger generations in China. The older generation held onto traditional customs like arranged marriages, multi-generational households, and strict gender roles, believing these practices were crucial to preserving cultural identity and social stability. They often viewed the wartime changes with skepticism and resistance. In contrast, the younger generation, shaped by the war's hardships, increasingly embraced new ways of life. Faced with economic challenges, many young people began to move away from traditional practices, pursuing love-based monogamous marriages, education, and career opportunities in the cities.

In rural areas, traditional social separation between men and women was common, with clear divisions in their roles. Women were expected to stay in domestic spaces or gather in all-female groups, while men would gather separately, often for work or socializing. At home, women took care of the household and children, while men worked and made decisions. Despite the war, these roles mostly remained, though the conflict slowly led to some change. As men went off to fight, women began working outside the home, taking on jobs that were once seen as men's work. Many also pursued education, with more women attending schools and training in nursing, teaching, and business. In larger cities like Shanghai and Beijing, educated men and women interacted more freely, especially in professional or academic settings, where traditional roles were less strict. These changes, driven by necessity, helped push society toward progress while still holding onto cultural traditions.

Marriage practices also changed during the war. Traditionally, Chinese men had multiple wives, with marriages arranged for economic or family reasons. However, as the war disrupted daily life, marriages became simpler, focusing on the bond between one man and one woman. This shift reflected a move toward more modern, equal relationships. Weddings, once grand and elaborate, became smaller and more practical due to the ongoing conflict. Couples prioritized unity over tradition, with the act of marriage itself taking precedence over large celebrations. The war brought about a blending of old customs and new influences, reshaping society's approach to marriage.

As the war disrupted society, China's class structure began to change as well. The urban elite, who were used to wealth and privilege, found themselves facing the same hardships as the working class, especially after many had to move to safer areas like Chongqing. Meanwhile, the working class, particularly women who started working in factories, farms, and hospitals, played a bigger role in the war effort, challenging old gender and class norms. The Communist Party's message of equality resonated with many, especially in rural areas, and more people began questioning the old power structures. This shift in attitude helped create greater social mobility and set the stage for political changes in the years that followed.

人民

駝峰空運始於 1942 年，當時緬甸遭日本佔領，切斷了中國的補給路線。美國陸軍航空隊（U.S. Army Air Force）將重要物資從印度飛越喜瑪拉雅山脈運往中國，幫助中國繼續對抗日本。中國人民則在修建機場跑道、提供地面支援和協助後勤工作方面發揮了關鍵的作用。後來，中國飛行員與美國飛行員聯合起來，組建了中美空軍混合團。這個空運行動對於在二戰期間維持盟軍在太平洋戰區的支援至關重要。

駝峰空運期間的中美合作

在駝峰空運期間，中國人民與美軍之間的合作並不限於後勤和航運安全，而是延伸到了一同用餐和日常互動等層面。中國勞動者經常被稱為「苦力」，他們在艱難的高海拔地區建造跑道和補給設施時甚為重要。在工具有限和條件惡劣的情況下，他們清理土地、整平地面，並建造倉庫和燃料庫等必要設施。當美國飛行員飛越險峻的喜馬拉雅山，向中國運送重要補給品的時候，他們依靠中國人在機場的支援來卸下和整備補給品。中美雙方的夥伴關係不僅存在於在實際作戰中，而也透過了一同飲食、工作的平凡日常建立了起來。

美軍和華工經常一起用餐，在戰爭的艱苦中培養出友誼。雖然美軍有配給的口糧可以食用，但有時並不足以應對惡劣的山區環境。熟悉傳統食物的中國當地人會與美軍分享米飯、蔬菜，偶爾也會分享肉類，幫助他們填飽肚子。有時候這些食物會在數英里之外準備好並運送給美軍，讓他們得以應付漫長而艱苦的旅途。不論是在路上或是在臨時休息站，他們只要找得到適合的地方就會用餐。這些共享餐點的經驗有助於彌合文化隔閡，也透過合作和相互支持緩解了語言障礙。

依靠技能生存

即使在戰爭的混亂中，中國的市集仍然熙熙攘攘，是充滿活力的中心地。由於傳統生計在戰爭期間受到破壞，小型生意便成了必要的謀生方法。在擁擠的市集裡，婦女們出售手工製作的圍巾，這些圍巾不僅實用，還展現出當地人的手藝和韌性。農民採集當地天然生長的水果和堅果，並將其販賣以維持生計，這成為戰爭期間糧食短缺時的重要營養來源。

市場不僅僅是一個交易場所，更是堅毅不屈的象徵。儘管戰爭肆虐，街角和空地上仍然充滿了武術家和雜技表演者的吆喝，他們表演古老的技藝以謀生。這些深深根源於中國傳統的技藝表演，為厭倦戰爭的人們帶來了短暫的驚奇和歡樂。對於賣藝者來說，在城鎮之間來回演出不僅僅是一種生存方式，也能藉此維持文化活力。

隨著許多家庭因戰爭而分崩離析，寫信人對於那些根本不識字或不會寫字的人們而言至關重要。有了他們撰寫書信，這些不會讀書寫字的民眾才得以彼此保持聯繫。與此同時，算命在中國向來有根深蒂固的傳統，在充滿不確定性的戰爭年代為人們提供慰藉和指引方向。這些服務在市場上的需求很大，讓失業的中國讀書人仍有辦法養家糊口，同時也為所有在戰時的黑暗中掙扎前行的中國人提供希望和指引。

男性外出打仗後，工廠和農場的工作由女性接手，在當地市場銷售商品。她們管理家庭、照顧兒童，並製作衣物出售。兒童在工廠打雜，收集木柴，甚至在田間和工廠工作。儘管生活艱苦，這些婦孺仍然表現出驚人的毅力，幫助他們的家庭克服戰時生活的挑戰。

救助貧民與孤兒

因為城市被摧毀、家庭四分五裂、經濟崩潰，乞丐在中國變得司空見慣。婦女、兒童和老人聚集在市集或街角，希望能夠求得食物或金錢。資源稀缺，家庭失散，導致乞討成為為數不多的生存方式之一。大量的乞丐反映出戰爭造成的普遍困境。

為了解決這個日益嚴重的問題，救世軍（Salvation Army）和其他組織一同為乞丐建造了營地。營地一次可容納多達 2000 人，並為那些飢寒交迫、無家可歸的人們提供了重要的支持。在警方的協助下，將乞丐集合起來，帶離公共租界的街道。在營地裡，他們至少能獲得溫飽，有竹製棚屋可以棲身。營地還附設學校、福音之家和工作坊，讓人們有機會重建人生，重拾尊嚴。

　　與此同時，孤兒院對於那些在戰爭中失去父母的兒童來說不可或缺。慈善組織為這些兒童提供住所、食物和安全感，讓他們在一片混亂之中仍然看得到希望和安定。孤兒院也提供教育，確保這些兒童即使經歷了創傷，但還是有機會學習和成長。對許多人而言，孤兒院是他們在戰爭期間唯一可以開始治癒身心創傷的地方，彷彿恢復了正常生活。

中國時尚的趨勢

　　二戰期間，由於國家面臨日本侵略以及內部鬥爭，中國的時尚風潮開始發生變化。長袍、馬褂、旗袍等傳統服裝仍然普遍，但戰時環境促成了服裝選擇的轉變。孫中山所創製的中山裝以其簡單實用的設計滿足了當時的需求，成為團結一致和堅忍不拔的象徵，因而大受歡迎。西式西裝也在城市精英中流行起來，被視為現代化和教養的象徵。帽子和鞋子的改變也隨之而來。男性以更為實用的中山帽取代了傳統的幞頭，與軍事風的中山裝相得益彰，而女性則選擇更簡單實用的頭巾。鞋類也變得更耐穿，男性偏愛軍靴，女性則選擇舒適實用的鞋子。服裝、帽子和鞋子的這些變化反映出中國試圖在維護傳統以及因應現代戰時世界的需求之間取得平衡。

　　髮型樣式也隨著這場廣泛的轉變而改變。傳統上，男性留長髮或是將其盤成頭髻，女性則將頭髮打理成精緻的高髻或是辮子。但隨著戰事的進展，特別是在城市裡，出現了更實用、簡化的髮型。男性開始偏好更短、更乾淨的髮型，這樣的髮型較容易打理，也適合軍事風的中山裝。女性也摒棄了複雜的髮型，選擇了更簡單、更短的髮型或是波浪捲，在戰時的環境下更為實用。這些服裝與髮型上的轉變，是中國嘗試現代化的同時，在不穩定的時期仍維持其文化根源的一部分。

中華文化的轉變

　　中國的上一代和下一代之間也出現了分歧。老一代人堅持傳統習俗，如包辦婚姻、多代同堂的家庭和嚴格的性別角色等等，認為這些習俗對於維護文化認同和社會穩定至關重要。他們經常對於戰時的變化投以懷疑和排斥的目光。相比之下，受戰爭困境影響的年輕一代則愈來愈接受新的生活方式。面對經濟挑戰，許多年輕人開始擺脫傳統習俗，追求以愛情為基礎的一夫一妻制婚姻，以及城市的教育與就業機會。

　　在農村地區，男女授受不親的傳統性別隔離仍然普遍，性別角色之間的分工明確。社會期望女性待在家中或是與清一色的女性聚集，而男性則通常為了工作或社交而另外聚會。在家裡，女性負責相夫教子，而男性則負責工作並做出決策。即使爆發了戰爭，這些性別角色規範大致上仍一成不變，但戰爭也慢慢促成了一些變化。隨著許多男性前往前線打仗，女性開始出外工作，接手了曾被視為專屬於男性的職業。許多女性也追求教育，體現在更多的婦女就學或是接受護理、教學和商業培訓。在上海和北平等大城市，受過教育的男女之間的互動更加自由，尤其是在專業或學術環境裡，傳統性別角色沒有那麼嚴格。這些由必要性所驅使的變革在維持文化傳統的同時，也推動了社會的進步。

　　在戰爭期間，婚姻習俗也發生了變化。傳統上，中國男人出於經濟或家庭因素，三妻四妾的情況不算罕見。然而隨著戰爭擾亂了日常生活，婚姻變得愈來愈單純，著重於一男一女之間的緊密關係。這種轉變反映出兩性關係邁向更現代化、平等的趨勢。由於戰火不斷，曾經盛大而繁複的婚禮變得更小巧而實際。夫妻比起傳統更加重視兩人間團結一心，而婚姻本身比大型婚宴更為重要。這場戰爭使舊習俗和新影響相互交融，重塑了社會對於婚姻的看法。

　　隨著戰爭擾亂社會，中國的階級結構也開始發生變化。原本享有財富和特權的城市精英發現自己與工人階級面臨相同的困境，尤其是在許多社會精英不得不遷徙到重慶等更安全的地區之後，這個現象更是明顯。與此同時，工人階級，尤其是開始在工廠、農場和醫院工作的女性，在戰爭中扮演了更重要的角色，挑戰舊有的性別和階級規範。尤其是在農村地區，共產黨的平等思想引起許多人的共鳴，也有愈來愈多人開始質疑舊有的權力結構。這種態度的轉變協助創造出更大的社會流動性，並為隨後幾年的政治變革奠定基礎。

An American radio team of the 64th Regiment were eating rice with their Chinese friends near Inkangahtawng in Myanmar. (May 16, 1944)

美軍第 64 團無線電小組正與他們的中國朋友在緬甸印康伽團（Inkangahtawng）附近用餐。

Date of Photo 時間：May 16, 1944
Credits 來源：美國國家檔案館 Photo Courtesy of National Archives

Chinese soldiers at the front in Myanmar were eating the meals that the cooks had brought from their kitchen 3 miles behind the frontline. (May 12, 1944)

在緬甸前線作戰的中國士兵,他們吃的飯是廚子從後方 3 英里的廚房帶過來的。

Date of Photo 時間：May 12, 1944
Credits 來源：美國國家檔案館 Photo Courtesy of National Archives

Chinese drivers were taking a break from repairing their vehicles to eat near Guiyang on Chongqing-Guiyang road. (Feb 18, 1945)

幾位中國司機在重慶至貴陽的公路上修車之餘，稍事休息並用餐。地點在貴陽附近。

Date of Photo 時間：February 18, 1945
Credits 來源：美國國家檔案館 Photo Courtesy of National Archives

In 1944, Chinese people were using handmade wheelbarrows to transport materials in building the military airport near Chengdu, China to support the Anti-Japanese war.

1944年,中國民眾正利用徒手製成的手推車載運物資到中國成都附近的軍用機場以支援抗日戰爭。

Date of Photo 時間:1944
Credits 來源:美國國家檔案館 Photo Courtesy of National Archives

A professional letter writer was writing a letter for his client in Guangzhou (Canton), China.

專門幫人寫信的男子正為他的客戶撰寫書信。拍攝地點是廣州。

Date of Photo 時間：不詳 N/A
Credits 來源：美國國家檔案館 Photo Courtesy of National Archives

A fortune teller in Guangzhou told his client, who wanted to know whether he should go to another city for a better job, the Chinese equivalent of "Go west, young Man".

廣州的一位算命先生告訴他的客戶該不該去另一座城市尋找更好的工作——如果是在美國西部拓荒時期，這大概就相當於那句有名的口號：「年輕人，往西部去吧！」

Date of Photo 時間：不詳 N/A
Credits 來源：美國國家檔案館 Photo Courtesy of National Archives

An old-fashioned fortune teller sat in front of the door surrounded by his tools of an *I Ching* set and a container of oracle sticks was waiting for clients, while a Chinese medical clinic advertisement was displayed on the side wall.

這位坐在門口等顧客的算命先生看來充滿舊中國的風味,身旁鋪滿了《易經》、籤筒等算命工具,旁邊的牆上則貼著中醫診所的廣告。

Date of Photo 時間:不詳 N/A
Credits 來源:美國國家檔案館 Photo Courtesy of National Archives

A Tibetan woman, wearing a typical costume of Tibet including fur-lined cap with ear flaps, came over the Himalayas to sell her hand woven tapes to the women of Darjeeling in the market.

一位圖博（藏族）婦女穿著典型的傳統服飾，包括帶耳蓋的毛皮襯帽，翻越喜馬拉雅山來到大吉嶺的市場上向婦女兜售她手工編織的帶子。

Date of Photo 時間：不詳 N/A
Credits 來源：美國國家檔案館 Photo Courtesy of National Archives

Vendors were selling peanuts in front of the gate of the temple of heaven. Looking closely, the gate had been heavily graffitied.

小販在天壇的門前兜售花生。仔細看的話,可以看到門上滿是塗鴉。

Date of Photo 時間:不詳 N/A
Credits 來源:美國國家檔案館 Photo Courtesy of National Archives

Two women were making firecrackers in a factory in Macau, during World War two.

二戰期間，兩位婦女正在澳門的工廠裡製造爆竹。

Date of Photo 時間：不詳 N/A
Credits 來源：美國國家檔案館 Photo Courtesy of National Archives

A young Chinese swordsman was performing in front of a crowd of spectators.

一位中國少年在觀眾面前表演耍劍。

Date of Photo 時間：不詳 N/A
Credits 來源：美國國家檔案館 Photo Courtesy of National Archives

A Shanghai policeman was taking two beggars to a Beggar Camp established by the Salvation Army in cooperation with several other organizations, where they were fed, cleaned, clothed, and housed in bamboo shacks.

一名上海警察正帶著兩名乞丐前往救世軍與其他幾個組織合作建立的乞丐收容所,在那裡他們至少可以獲得溫飽,好好洗個澡,並且有竹棚可以棲身。

Date of Photo 時間:不詳 N/A
Credits 來源:美國國家檔案館 Photo Courtesy of National Archives

Taoist wedding musicians, dressed in ceremonial robes, were preparing to perform. The man on the left was holding a *dongxiao*, which is a vertical bamboo flute while the man on the right was holding a *sheng* which is a Chinese reed pipe.

身著道袍的道教婚禮樂師正準備演出。左邊的人拿著一支竹製洞簫，右邊那一位則拿著中國的簧管樂器「笙」。

Date of Photo 時間：不詳 N/A
Credits 來源：美國國家檔案館 Photo Courtesy of National Archives

A new-style wedding in Chongqing, the wartime capital of China, featured the bride in a *Qipao* and the groom in a Sun Yat-sen suit, while guests weared a mix of traditional Chinese clothes (*Changpao/Qipao*), Sun Yat-sen suit, or Western-style suits.

位於中國戰時首都重慶的一場新式婚禮,其中新娘穿著旗袍,新郎穿著中山裝,賓客的服裝樣式則是新舊夾雜,有長袍(旗袍)、中山裝或是西裝等等。

Date of Photo 時間:不詳 N/A
Credits 來源:美國國家檔案館 Photo Courtesy of National Archives

A traditional Chinese-style gathering in public typically featured women and children on one side while men gathered on the other side. This separation reflected longstanding cultural norms and social structures, where men and women had distinct roles in public life.

在中國傳統的公共聚會上，通常是婦女與兒童站在一邊，男性則站在另一邊。這種男女有別的狀態反映出長久以來的文化規範和社會結構，其中男性和女性在公共生活中扮演著不同的角色。

Date of Photo 時間：不詳 N/A
Credits 來源：美國國家檔案館 Photo Courtesy of National Archives

Chinese drivers stopped for a meal along the Burma Road. They were called "Hell Drivers" because their trucks were constantly in danger of being bombed or machine-gunned by the Japanese planes.

中國司機在滇緬公路上某處停下來用餐。由於他們的卡車總是面臨被日軍轟炸或是用機槍掃射的危險,因而有「地獄司機」之稱。

Date of Photo 時間:不詳 N/A
Credits 來源:美國國家檔案館 Photo Courtesy of National Archives

On the afternoon and evening of June 6, crowds of Chongqing residents watched news bulletins for the latest information about the Allied landings in France.

1944年6月6日的下午與傍晚,重慶居民聚集在名為「每日戰況」的公佈欄前面閱讀最新消息,關心盟軍在法國諾曼第海灘進行登陸作戰的軍情。

Date of Photo 時間:June 6, 1944
Credits 來源:美國國家檔案館 Photo Courtesy of National Archives

A Mongolian warrior was holding an extraordinary bow and carrying a quiver full of arrows showcasing a form of weaponry and tradition deeply rooted in the nomadic culture of the steppes. Bows and arrows were still used during the war in the east, although they were dying out.

一位蒙古戰士手持一把長弓，背著裝滿弓箭的箭袋，展現了一種深深根植於草原游牧文化的武器裝備和傳統。儘管弓箭在當年已逐漸式微，但東方的戰場上仍有人使用。

Date of Photo 時間：不詳 N/A
Credits 來源：美國國家檔案館 Photo Courtesy of National Archives

This image is a typical portrait of "Chao mu" (grandmother), representing the Chinese farmland. She tills the soil with primitive tools, working alongside the bases and modern mechanical equipment of Major General Chenault's 14th Air Force in their fight against a common enemy.

這幅影像是典型的「祖母像」，是中國農村的象徵。她仍利用原始工具耕耘土地，與其並肩作戰的是陳納德少將麾下第14航空隊，他們則是靠基地與現代機械裝備抗敵。

Date of Photo 時間：不詳 N/A
Credits 來源：美國國家檔案館 Photo Courtesy of National Archives

An elderly man in Inner Mongolia enjoyed a moment of peace as he sat before a tent, smoking a long pipe.

內蒙古的一位長者坐在營帳前抽著長菸斗,享受片刻的寧靜。

Date of Photo 時間:不詳 N/A
　　Credits 來源:美國國家檔案館 Photo Courtesy of National Archives

This is a portrait of a typical elderly Lama priest in Tibet with a long white beard and distinctive tall hat.

這是一幅典型的圖博（藏族）老年喇嘛肖像，他留著白色長鬚，戴著獨特的高帽。

Date of Photo 時間：不詳 N/A
Credits 來源：美國國家檔案館 Photo Courtesy of National Archives

CITY

On August 15th, 1945, Japan announced its surrender, which marked the end of one of the most devastating chapters in human history. The war was over for most of the world–but for China–the true impact of this announcement had just begun. Over one million Japanese soldiers were still stationed across the vast region of China. The end of the war created a new and urgent challenge: how to ensure the safe surrender of these troops and most importantly how to guide China through the complexities of transitioning from war to peace.

The American Hand

The Chinese people had been battered and scarred by the years of brutal invasion and occupation. The Chinese Military and government were exhausted from years of internal strife and foreign invasion. Coordinating such a large-scale operation alone would have been a monumental challenge. Luckily, the United States stepped in to provide crucial assistance.

After completing their campaigns in the Pacific, the American Army extended a helping hand to the Chinese as a partner during this challenging transition. The role of the American army in this task was clear: to offer logistical and advisory support to ensure a peaceful surrender of Japanese forces and the smooth withdrawal of Japanese troops from China. The American army helped with the planning and execution of the surrender ceremony, which ensured that Japanese soldiers knew exactly how to lay down their weapons and return to their homeland. Additionally, they also provided vital logistical support to China, which ensured that the food, supplies, and transportation were available to manage the Japanese troops effectively. By facilitating a smooth surrender process, the Americans aimed to minimize potential conflicts between Chinese factions during the post-war period.

A Fragile Peace

As the Japanese forces began their journey home, China faced a monumental task of healing. The Chinese military, assisted by American advisors, would now begin the long process of stabilizing the country. The country, scarred by years of war, was left in ruins — infrastructure had been destroyed, cities shattered, and a generation wounded by the ravages of violence and deprivation.

The American forces remained on the ground for a time, lending their assistance in the rebuilding effort, working to ensure that the transition to peace would not unravel. The surrender of Japanese forces on Chinese soil may have marked the official end of the war in that region, but for China, the true work of reconciliation and recovery was just beginning.

The collaboration between the United States and China during this pivotal moment was a testament to a shared desire for peace. However, it also underscored the complexities of post-war Asia, where political divisions, old wounds, and new struggles for power would soon emerge. The journey toward lasting peace would prove to be long and fraught with challenges,

Priceless Aerial Memories

Between September and November of 1945, the U.S. Navy's Seventh Fleet, stationed aboard the *Antietam* aircraft carrier, conducted escort and patrol missions along China's eastern coast. During this time, the 89th Naval Air Wing captured invaluable aerial photographs that documented a pivotal moment in history. These images, taken during the peacekeeping operations over China's airspace, showcase a range of key locations, including Beijing, Tianjin, Shanghai, Qingdao, Lushun, Dalian, Tongzhou, Changli, Tangshan, Qinhuangdao, Tanggu, Jimo, Jiaozhou, and the surrounding areas.

The photographs offer a rare and intimate view of China during this transitional period, capturing the classic landscapes, cities, people, and scenes of the time. Each image serves as a microcosm of China in 1945 — a country on the brink of peace, yet still deeply marked by the impacts of war. These priceless aerial photographs provide an invaluable glimpse into the historical moment when China, and the world, were forever changing.

Beijing

In 1945, Beijing was filled with the joy of victory and resonated with the sounds of a hard-earned peace after Japan's surrender. These photos, taken through the portholes of US military aircraft, offer a rare glimpse of a city on the cusp of transformation. One particular image taken near the heart of the city around Chang'an Street and Zhongnanhai captures a fleeting moment of celebration. In the photo, a temporary paper-colored archway stands proudly in front of Xinhua Gate, hastily built as a symbol of victory. The archway, though simple, held deep meaning for the people of Beijing. For centuries, such structures had been erected during important festivals and events, serving as a way to honor significant moments and mark the passage of time.

These photos captured the historical look of Beijing and its surrounding rural areas. Among the most iconic was the view of Chang'an Street, often called China's "No. 1 street." Stretching for miles through the heart of the city, it stood as a symbol of Beijing's historical significance and central role. Nearby, Zhongnanhai represented both continuity and change. Once an imperial garden, it had transformed into the center of China's political power, housing the offices and residences of the nation's leaders. Another striking image offered a close-up of the Fairy Island Palace in Yingtai, surrounded by the South China Sea of Zhongnanhai. Once a private retreat for emperors and the site where Emperor Guangxu met his tragic end, it was now a meeting place for national leaders.

As the plane approached the Forbidden City, the view shifted to the grand imperial palace, once the center of Chinese power. Below, U.S. military vehicles were stationed in a vast square, a reminder of the Allied forces' support for the Chinese army. The area had transformed into a logistical hub for the transfer of supplies and equipment. On October 10, 1945, the surrender ceremony of the Japanese invaders in North China was held in the Forbidden City. Military bugles sounded from the peak of Jingshan Mountain, and salutes were fired at the Hall of Supreme Harmony, the main venue of the event. Over 10,000 Chinese citizens, along with representatives from the United States, Britain, the Soviet Union, and other nations, gathered to celebrate the victory. The Forbidden City, once a palace for emperors, had now become an accessible symbol of China's new chapter in history.

Flew further into the suburbs of Beijing, the landscape shifted. In the distance, the Temple of Heaven rose above the trees. Surrounded by historic pinewoods, the temple stood at the center of Chinese cosmogony, embodying the deep belief in the harmony between earth and heaven. The emperor, as the son of heaven, had long played a pivotal role in maintaining this cosmic balance. Now, as the city embraced a new era, the Temple of Heaven stood as a silent witness to the unfolding changes.

The Great Wall of China is winding its way through the rugged mountains to the north. The wall, an enduring symbol of China's strength and resilience, stood as it always had—ancient, unyielding, and majestic. Despite the passage of time and the challenges of war, the Great Wall remained a constant, a testament to the enduring spirit of the Chinese people.

Tianjin

When Japan announced its surrender on August 15, 1945, the people of Tianjin cheered in tears of joy, celebrating with fireworks. Following a local tradition, the people of Tianjin would eat noodles to mark a happy occasion. That afternoon, crowds of people carrying bags rushed from one shop to another, eager to buy noodles. To help those in poor, some shops offered noodles for free. In their own unique way, the people of Tianjin released the years of frustration and suffering they had endured. On October 6, 1945, Chinese officials, alongside representatives from the United States Army, accepted Japan's surrender in Tianjin.

The aerial photos capture both the urban landscape and the surrounding rural areas. One city-view picture showed Central Park, once the French Park in the French Concession of Tianjin, which is a prominent landmark in the city. Located at the heart of Tianjin, it was once surrounded by the residences of notable individuals. Despite many changes over time, the basic road layout and several historic buildings have been preserved today. Another picture showed East Street, which is one of the commercial centers in Tianjin. East Street is the home to the Wuhe Department Store and renowned Chinese brands like Zheng Xing De Tea Shop, Nei Lian Sheng Shoe Shop, and numerous pharmacies. The crowded streets and trams reflected the city's prosperity right after the war.

Flying southeast, Taku is located about 20 kilometers from Tianjin, near the mouth of the Haihe River where it flows into the Bohai Sea. Taku was historically significant as the site of the Taku Forts, which played a crucial role during the late Qing Dynasty, the First Opium War, and in the defense of Tianjin during the Second World War against Japan. This rural area, with its factories surrounded by farmland and ships being transferred along the river, was poised for a promising future.

Shanghai

In 1945, Shanghai stood as the largest city in the Far East. When Japan's emperor declared the defeat of his nation, the streets erupted in celebration. People raised the flags of China, the United States, Britain, and the Soviet Union, honoring the monumental victory shared with the Allies. Shanghai businessmen celebrated in their own way. Many stores launched big sales, teahouses offered free tea, and pubs served free wine. Many events were held, and huge signboards and advertisements in stores also displayed slogans celebrating the victory. In November 1945, Shanghai citizens spontaneously organized a rickshaw rally to celebrate the victory of the Anti-Japanese War, in which a Chinese rickshaw driver pulled a female American soldier, racing fast and even winning prizes.

To ensure a smooth transition following Japan's surrender, U.S. Navy warships, medical ships, and British warships were anchored in the Huangpu River. Small fishing boats crowded around the warships, with Chinese vendors on board selling goods to the U.S. military. Along the river, the Bund was lined with high-rise buildings, a true reflection of Shanghai's development at the time. Today, many of the classic buildings, showcasing a variety of architectural styles, still stand on the Bund. These structures have witnessed Shanghai's history and the city's transformation over the years.

Other Cities near East coast

Flying along the eastern coast of China, these aerial photos captured several cities, including Tangshan, Qinhuangdao, Qingdao, and Yantai. The damage from the war is evident in the shattered buildings and destroyed railways. The ancient cities with their city walls and grid-like streets reflect the enduring legacy of traditional urban planning, emphasizing the importance of defense, order, and structure in these civilizations.

Eighty years after the Marco Polo Bridge incident, these cities have undergone tremendous change. However, the aerial photos from 1945 remain a precious historical record. The clarity of the images allows viewers to almost feel as if they are stepping back into that moment in time, connecting with a period of history that shaped the future of these cities.

城市

日本於 1945 年 8 月 15 日宣布投降，人類歷史上最具毀滅性的篇章終於畫下句點。對世界上大多數國家來說，戰爭已經結束；但是對中國來說，這個宣告的真正影響才剛剛開始。仍有超過 100 萬日本士兵駐紮在廣大的中國各地。終戰帶來了一個全新且緊迫的挑戰：如何確保這些部隊的投降過程安全，以及最重要的是如何引領中國度過從戰爭到和平的這段過渡時期。

美國的援手

　　多年的殘酷侵略和佔領使得中國人民遍體鱗傷。多年的內部糾紛和外敵入侵也使中國軍隊和政府疲憊不堪。獨自協調如此大規模的行動將會是可觀的挑戰。幸運的是，美國在此時介入並提供了關鍵性的援助。

　　美軍在完成太平洋戰區的戰事以後向中國伸出援手，與中國在這個充滿挑戰的過渡時期攜手合作。美軍在這項任務中的角色很明確：提供後勤和諮詢支援，以確保日軍和平投降並順利撤出中國。美軍協助策劃和執行投降儀式，以確保日本士兵確切明白如何放下武器並返回家園。此外，他們還為中國提供了重要的後勤支援，確保了食品、物資和交通運輸能夠有效地用於管理日本軍隊。透過推動順利的投降過程，美國人的目標是盡量減少戰後中國各政軍派系之間的潛在衝突。

脆弱的和平

　　隨著日本軍隊開始返國，中國也面臨著癒合國內傷痕的龐大任務。中國軍方在美國顧問的協助下，開始了讓國家穩定下來的漫長歷程。多年的戰爭使這個國家傷痕累累，到處都是斷垣殘壁——基礎設施被毀，城市支離破碎，一整個世代的中國人因為暴力和物資匱乏的摧殘而身心飽受創傷。

　　美國軍隊在當地停留了一段時間，協助重建工作，努力確保往和平的過渡進程不會瓦解。日軍在中國土地上投降可能標誌著這個地區的戰爭已正式結束，但對於中國而言，真正去推動和解與恢復的工作才剛剛開始。

在這個關鍵時刻，中美兩國之間的合作證明了雙方同樣渴望和平。然而，這也突顯了戰後亞洲局勢的錯綜複雜，政治分歧、歷史舊傷和新的權力鬥爭很快就會出現。事後證明，邁向長久和平的道路漫長且荊棘遍佈。

無價的空中回憶

1945 年 9 月至 11 月，美國海軍第七艦隊駐紮於安提頓號航空母艦（USS *Antietam*），在中國東部沿海執行護航和巡邏任務。在此期間，第 89 海軍航空聯隊拍攝了寶貴的航拍照片，記錄歷史上的關鍵時刻。這些照片是在中國領空執行維和行動期間拍攝的，入境的包括許多重要地點，包括北平、天津、上海、青島、旅順、大連、通州、昌黎、唐山、秦皇島、塘沽、即墨、膠州以及周邊地區。

這些相片讓我們得以看見中國在這段過渡期間罕見而親近的一面，捕捉了當時的經典景觀、城市、人物和場景。每張照片都是 1945 年中國的縮影——讓我們得以將一個即將邁向和平，卻仍然深受戰爭影響的國家收入眼底。這批珍貴的航拍照讓我們得以窺探中國與世界永遠改變的歷史性時刻，彷彿無價之寶。

北平

1945 年，北平充滿了勝利的喜悅，與日本投降後來之不易的和平之聲共鳴。這些照片是從美國軍機的舷窗拍攝出去的，讓我們得以一窺這個處於變革尖端的城市，非常難得。其中一張照片攝於長安街和中南海附近的市中心地帶，捕捉到了轉瞬即逝的慶祝時刻。在照片中，一座臨時且匆忙建成的紙色牌坊驕傲地矗立於新華門前，以作為勝利的象徵。這座牌坊雖然簡單，但對北平民眾而言意義深遠。幾個世紀以來，人們都會在重要的節日和活動中搭建這樣的建築物，以作為紀念重要時刻和標誌時間流逝的一種方式。

這些照片捕捉了北平及周圍農村地區的歷史風貌。其中最具代表性的是常被稱為「中國第一街」的長安街。綿延數英里的長安街穿過市中心，是北平歷史意義和中心地位的象徵。鄰近的中南海同時代表著延續與改變。中南海曾經是一座御苑，而現在已搖身一變成為中國的政治權力中心，是國家領導人辦公室和官邸的所在地。另一張引人注目的圖片是位於瀛台的蓬萊閣特寫，四周由中南海的南海包圍。瀛台曾是清朝歷代皇帝的隱居處所，也是光緒帝遭長期幽禁後悲慘駕崩的地方，現在則是國家領導人的聚會場所。

當飛機接近紫禁城時，視線轉移到了這座宏偉的皇城，那裡曾經是中國的權力中心。底下，美軍車輛停駐在廣闊的廣場上，彷彿讓我們不能忘卻盟軍對於中國軍隊的支持。這塊區域已經轉變成了物資和設備轉運的物流樞紐。1945年10月10日，接受華北侵華日軍投降的儀式在紫禁城舉行。軍號從景山山頂響起，禮炮則在主會場太和殿響起。超過1萬名中國公民與來自美國、英國、蘇聯等國家的代表齊聚一堂，慶祝勝利。紫禁城曾經是帝王的宮殿，現在已成為中國歷史新篇章中平易近人的象徵。

再往北平郊區飛去，景觀發生了變化。遠處，天壇聳立在樹林之中。天壇被歷史悠久的松樹林環繞，是中國宇宙觀的中心，體現了天地和諧的深厚信仰。皇帝作為天子，長期以來在維護這種宇宙的平衡中扮演中樞的角色。現在，隨著這座城市迎向新的時代，天壇默默地見證著正在發生的變化。

中國的萬里長城在北方崎嶇的群山中蜿蜒前行。這道長城是中國國力和堅毅的永恆象徵，它一如既往地屹立著——古老、不屈、雄偉。儘管經歷了滄海桑田和戰爭的挑戰，長城依然屹立不倒，見證中國人民永垂不朽的精神。

天津

　　1945 年 8 月 15 日，日本宣佈投降的時候，天津民眾歡呼雀躍、喜極而泣，並燃放煙火慶祝。按照當地的傳統，天津人會吃麵來慶祝此一喜事。那天下午，一群群天津人拿著袋子從一家商店衝到另一家商店，人人都想搶購麵條。為了幫助貧困民眾，有些商店免費提供麵食。天津人民以自己獨特的方式，釋放了他們多年來忍受的挫折和苦難。1945 年 10 月 6 日，中國官員與美國陸軍代表在天津接受了日軍投降。

　　這些航拍照片捕捉了城市景觀和周圍的農村地區。其中一張城市景觀照片顯示了中心公園，它曾是天津法租界的法國公園，是這座城市的著名地標。中心公園位於天津市中心，四周曾經都是知名人士的宅邸。儘管這一帶隨著歷史的演進而有許多變化，但基本的道路佈局和幾座歷史建築至今仍留存下來。另一張照片顯示的是東馬路，它是天津的商業中心之一。東馬路是五和百貨商場與正興德茶莊、內聯陞鞋業等中國知名品牌和眾多藥店的所在地。擁擠的街道和電車反映出城市在戰後的繁榮發展。

　　向東南飛去，大沽距離天津約 20 公里，鄰近海河流入渤海的入海口。作為大沽炮台的所在地，大沽具有重要的歷史意義；在清朝末年、鴉片戰爭以及二戰的抗日作戰期間，大沽炮台在天津的防禦中發揮了關鍵作用。這個農村地帶有農田包圍工廠，船舶沿著河道往來，前景一片光明。

上海

　　上海在 1945 年躍升成為遠東最大的城市。當日本天皇宣佈他的國家戰敗時，街道上一片歡騰。人們紛紛升起中國、美國、英國和蘇聯的旗幟，慶祝與同盟國共同取得的巨大勝利。上海商人也以自己的方式慶祝。許多商店開始大促銷，茶館免費提供茶水，酒館免費提供葡萄酒。城裡舉辦了許多活動，商店裡的巨大招牌和廣告也打出了慶祝勝利的口號。1945 年 11 月，上海市民自發組織了人力車大會以慶祝抗日戰爭的勝利，其中一名中國人力車夫拉著一名美國女兵競速，甚至贏得了獎品。

為了確保日本投降後的順利交接，美國海軍軍艦、醫療船和英國軍艦都停泊在黃浦江。小漁船擠在軍艦周圍，船上的中國商販向美軍兜售商品。外灘的一棟棟高樓大廈沿著河岸排列，確實反映出上海當時的發展。今天，當中的許多經典建築仍然矗立在外灘，展現出各式各樣的建築風格。這些建築見證上海的歷史和這座城市多年來的轉變。

東海沿岸附近的其他城市

美軍軍機沿著中國東海岸飛行之際拍攝航空照，拍下了唐山、秦皇島、青島和煙臺等若干城市。從斷垣殘壁和被摧毀的鐵路來看，戰爭造成的破壞顯而易見。古老的城牆和網格狀的街道反映出傳統都市規劃的永恆影響，強調了防禦、秩序和結構等要素在這些文明中的重要性。

在盧溝橋事變八十年之後的現代，這些城市已歷經了巨變。然而，1945 年的航拍照片仍是珍貴的歷史記錄。清晰的影像讓那個時代躍然紙上，看著照片的人彷彿也置身於那一段形塑出城市未來的歷史時期。

Zhongnanhai and Chang'an Street in Beijing.
北平的中南海與長安街。

Date of Photo 時間：September 4, 1945
Credits 來源：美國國家檔案館 Photo Courtesy of National Archives

Fairy Island Palace in Yingtai of Zhongnanhai, Beijing.

北平中南海瀛台島上的蓬萊閣。

Date of Photo 時間：September 4, 1945
Credits 來源：美國國家檔案館 Photo Courtesy of National Archives

Forbidden City, Beijing.

北平紫禁城。

Date of Photo 時間：October 3, 1945
Credits 來源：美國國家檔案館 Photo Courtesy of National Archives

Temple of Heaven and Altar to Heaven, Beijing.

北平天壇，還有天壇裡的圜丘。

Date of Photo 時間：October 13, 1945
Credits 來源：美國國家檔案館 Photo Courtesy of National Archives

Great Wall of China near Beijing.

北平附近的萬里長城。

Date of Photo 時間：October 3, 1945
Credits 來源：美國國家檔案館 Photo Courtesy of National Archives

Northeast corner of East Street in Tianjin.

天津東馬路東北角。

Date of Photo 時間：October 3, 1945
Credits 來源：美國國家檔案館 Photo Courtesy of National Archives

Central Park (Former French Park) and French Concession in Tianjin.

中心公園（原法國公園）與天津法租界。

Date of Photo 時間：October 1, 1945
Credits 來源：美國國家檔案館 Photo Courtesy of National Archives

Taku district in Tianjin.

天津大沽地區。

Date of Photo 時間：October 3, 1945
Credits 來源：美國國家檔案館 Photo Courtesy of National Archives

A US NAVY aircraft was flying over the Huangpu River in Shanghai. The bund was lined with tall high-rise buildings, reflecting Shanghai's development at the time.

一架美國海軍軍機飛越上海黃浦江的上空。外灘河濱地區高樓大廈林立,反映出當時已蓬勃發展的上海。

Date of Photo 時間:September 28, 1945
Credits 來源:美國國家檔案館 Photo Courtesy of National Archives

U.S. Navy warships, medical ships, and British warships were anchored in the Huangpu River, Shanghai.

美國海軍軍艦、醫療船和英國軍艦都下錨停泊在上海黃浦江。

Date of Photo 時間：September 28, 1945
Credits 來源：美國國家檔案館 Photo Courtesy of National Archives

First Public School in Dalian built by Japanese - Fushimidai Public School and its surroundings.

伏見台公學堂是日本在大連建造的第一所公立學校,圖為學校與其周遭地區。

Date of Photo 時間:September 4, 1945
Credits 來源:美國國家檔案館 Photo Courtesy of National Archives

The railway station in Tangshan, near the Kailuan Coal Mine and surrounded by a small town and farms, served as a key transportation hub for delivering coal across China.

唐山的火車站鄰近開灤煤礦,周圍有一個小鎮與眾多農莊,該站是向全中國運送煤炭的重要交通樞紐。

Date of Photo 時間:October 4, 1945
Credits 來源:美國國家檔案館 Photo Courtesy of National Archives

A walled city near Tsingtao, a traditional Chinese town with city walls and a moat, features neat streets running from north to south and west to east.

青島附近的即墨城,這個傳統中式古城有城牆和護城河,城內的棋盤狀街道都是南北向或東西向,井然有序。

Date of Photo 時間:September 29, 1945
Credits 來源:美國國家檔案館 Photo Courtesy of National Archives

Cangkou is the largest industrial district in Qingdao, home to many time-honored factories like Sun Rubber and Huaxin Cotton Mill.

滄口是青島最大的工業區，有許多歷史悠久的工廠，像是太陽膠皮廠與華新紗廠。

Date of Photo 時間：September 10, 1945
Credits 來源：美國國家檔案館 Photo Courtesy of National Archives

CONCLUSION

The story of China at war—from the early 1930s through to the end of World War II—is one of tremendous transformation, heartbreaking sacrifice, and indomitable resilience. Japan's early invasions of Manchuria and the establishment of puppet regimes set in motion a series of humanitarian, economic, and military mobilizations that reshaped the nation. This conclusion weaves together strands of civilian relief, economic aid, military cooperation, cultural fusion, and the fortunes of refugees, women, children, and peasants to demonstrate how the travails of war gave rise to a modern China.

Amidst generalized destruction and despair, an extensive array of grassroots associations, charitable societies, and foreign partners mobilized to assist the war-torn population. When both government and military aid from the United States was curtailed by economic problems at home and a general mood of isolationism in the early 1930s, private foundations filled the breach. The organizations built hospitals, orphanages, and schools, offering both immediate relief and hope for the future. The formation of the American Federation to Aid China in 1940, for instance, was a deep humanitarian commitment that reached across borders and cultural divides in support of China's resistance.

Wartime economic assistance was no less complex and critical. Carefully negotiated financial agreements, like the "tung oil loan" and the "Tungsten Sand Loan Contract," provided China with urgently required materials and supplies, although the agreements were qualified by the delicate balance between supporting a distant ally and maintaining neutrality in a polarized world. The extension of Lend-Lease to China in 1941 was a watershed; this enormous aid package, totaling over $1.335 billion by the war's end, supplied vital war material while manifesting a firm commitment to collective defense against the Axis.

Military collaboration between the United States and China developed from pragmatic necessity into a genuine personal alliance. Following the bombing of Pearl Harbor, American soldiers, engineers, and aviators joined forces with Chinese soldiers—most notably the Flying Tigers—in a shared struggle against Japanese aggression. Beyond the battlefield, Chinese workers and soldiers assisted in supporting crucial logistical efforts, such as constructing airfields and helping to support the treacherous Hump Airlift operation. In these joint operations, airmen from both nations risked life and limb, forging bonds that would influence post-war relations and illustrate the deep, personal ties that were tempered in the crucible of war.

The human cost of war was starkly apparent in the refugee crisis that gripped the nation. Millions of citizens, uprooted from cities like Nanjing, Shanghai, and Beijing, undertook perilous journeys to escape the ravages of war. These travels—often on foot, in crowded trains, or through makeshift shelters—exposed individuals to starvation, disease, and relentless hardship. The refugee condition was not some abstract statistic but a daily reality, vividly delineated by the sprawling shantytowns and treacherous highways, where families were torn apart and survival was an everyday ordeal.

Key urban centers such as Wuhan and Kunming were microcosms of wartime hardship and survival. Kunming in particular grew both as a strategic hub and as a bastion of cultural renaissance behind the enemy lines. Despite the pressures of rushed urbanization, social conflict between old residents and incoming refugees, and the enormous weight of infrastructural pressures, the city became an oasis where military planning, education, and cultural life intersected. The founding of National Southwestern Associated University—the Beijing University, Qinghua University, and Nankai University consortium—in Kunming was the stubborn refusal to allow learning and intellectual growth to fall prey to adversity.

In the rural areas of China, which occupied nearly 80 percent of the nation, the problems were equally daunting but of a different nature. Peasants endured economic exploitation, forced labor, and war's destruction as fields were ruined and ways of life were disrupted. Yet their knowledge of the local terrain energized an active resistance. Peasant fighters and guerrilla militias waged ambushes, sabotage, and other insurgent activities, forming the paradox of vulnerable victim and primary agent of resistance.

The impact of war on women and children also identifies the revolutionary nature of the period. As conventional gender roles disintegrated under the stress of war, women assumed greater roles within the labor force, police force, education, and manual labor, thereby challenging social norms. Though economic deprivation and social tensions caused issues such as sexual harassment and wage disparities, the war experience laid the groundwork for significant, lasting changes in gender relations. For children, the war was a profound rite of passage—highlighted by the pain of separation, loss of innocence, and the harsh dictates of survival—yet disrupted by periodic bursts of spontaneous joy through street games, backyard plays, and the collective song of cultural festivities.

This era also witnessed a unique cultural exchange, as Chinese and American traditions fused with one another in an attempt to foster understanding and unity. Common acts—such as sharing bread—became symbolic of the bridge between two worlds, demonstrating humanity's inclination to seek out common ground even amidst war.

As the war terminated with the surrender of Japan in 1945, China faced the daunting task of transitioning from total war to reconciliation and reconstruction. U.S. military assistance, in the form of logistic and advisory missions, helped facilitate the orderly withdrawal of Japanese forces, while aerial photography of the U.S. Navy's Seventh Fleet documented this transition period. The common deprivations of the war laid the foundations for political realignments, most notably the emergence of the Communist Party, and accelerated the social and cultural changes that propelled China's remarkable post-war modernization.

Essentially, the legacy of wartime China is a mixture of sacrifice, resilience, and reinvention—a narrative where the struggles of ordinary people catalyzed monumental change and set the stage for the modern Chinese state.

結語

從 1930 年代初期到二戰結束的這段時期，是一段中國對抗日本入侵的奮鬥史。當中有著巨大的轉變、令人心碎的犧牲還有不屈不撓的意志。從日本初期入侵滿洲並建立傀儡政權開始，在中國引發了一系列人道救援、經濟和軍事方面的動員，並重塑了國家。本書結語將結合民間救濟、經濟援助、軍事合作、文化融合與難民、婦女、兒童和農民的命運，以展示戰爭的艱辛如何造就了現代中國。

在普遍的破壞和絕望之中，眾多基層協會、慈善組織和外國合作夥伴動員起來，幫助飽受戰爭蹂躪的中國人民。1930 年代初期，美國政府和軍方的援助因國內經濟問題和孤立主義彌漫而受限，此時私人基金會填補了這個缺口。這些組織興建醫院、孤兒院和學校，提供了即時的救濟，讓人們對未來懷抱希望。例如，1940 年成立的「美國援華聯合會」（American Federation to Aid China）就展現出人道奉獻的堅決意志，跨越了國界和文化的藩籬，為中國對日抗戰展開支援。

戰時經濟援助的複雜性和關鍵性也不遑多讓。《桐油借款》和《鎢砂借款合約》等雖是謹慎談判下產生的金融協議，其實處處受到掣肘，因為美方一方面想支援遠方盟友，又想在兩極敵對的世界裡維持中立，不過這些協議仍為中國提供了急需的物資與補給品。1941 年讓《租借法案》適用於中國是一個分水嶺——這個龐大的援助計劃在終戰時總計超過 13.35 億美元，在提供重要戰爭物資的同時，也體現了集體防禦以對抗軸心國的堅定承諾。

中美之間的軍事合作最初只是出於必要的務實需求，到了後來卻發展成為了真正直達個人層級的同盟。珍珠港事件後，美國軍人、工程師和飛行員與中國軍方攜手合作（其中最著名的莫過於飛虎隊），共同抵抗日本侵略。在戰場之外，中國工人和士兵協助支援關鍵的後勤工作，例如建造機場，以及協助支援險象環生的駝峰空運行動。在這些聯合行動中，來自兩國的飛行員冒著生命危險，建立起足以影響戰後關係的紐帶，刻劃出在戰爭的試煉中鍛造出的深厚個人關係。

在籠罩全國的難民危機中，戰爭的人道代價顯現得淋漓盡致。南京、上海和北平等城市的千千萬萬居民背井離鄉，為了躲避戰爭的蹂躪而踏上了危機四伏的逃難路程。人們經常在徒步、乘坐擁擠的火車或是在臨時庇護所駐留的旅程裡，暴露在飢餓、疾病和無情的困苦之中。難民的處境並非僅僅是紙面上的抽象統計數字而已，而是他們每天切切實實的實際情況，在蔓生的棚屋區和危險的公路上生動上演。在那裡，家庭四分五裂，生存成了日復一日的折磨。

武漢和昆明等主要城市中心地帶是戰時困境和求生的縮影。尤其是昆明既成為戰略樞紐，也是後方文化復興的堡壘。儘管面臨急遽都市化的壓力、原有居民與新移民之間的社會衝突，以及基礎建設的巨大壓力，昆明仍成為了軍事規劃、教育與文化生活相互交集的綠洲。北京大學、清華大學和南開大學在昆明聯合創立的西南聯大，堅定拒絕讓學習和學術發展成為戰時逆境下的犧牲品。

在佔中國面積將近80％的農村地區，所面臨的問題同樣艱巨，性質卻截然不同。農民忍受經濟剝削、強迫勞動以及造成田地被摧毀、生活方式被擾亂的戰爭破壞。然而，他們憑著對於當地地形瞭若指掌而積極發起抗日行動。農民民兵和游擊隊員伏擊日軍、執行破壞任務和其他起義行動，形成了他們同屬脆弱的受害者還有主要反抗者的雙重矛盾身份。

戰爭對婦女和兒童的影響也彰顯出這段時期的革命性質。隨著傳統的性別角色在戰爭壓力下瓦解，婦女在勞力、警察、教育和體力勞動中發揮了更重大的作用，從而挑戰了社會規範。儘管經濟匱乏和社會緊張導致了性騷擾和工資差距等問題，戰爭經驗仍為性別關係中重大且持久的變化奠定了基礎。對於兒童來說，抗日戰爭是一種深刻的成人禮：這突顯在他們被迫承受與家人失散的痛苦、失去童真，以及求生過程中的苛刻；但仍不時穿插著街頭嬉戲、後院戲曲和文化節慶的集體歌聲，讓人不自覺地感到愉悅。

隨著中美傳統相互交融，藉此試圖促進彼此間的理解與團結，這個時代也見證了獨特的文化交流。分食麵包等共享的舉動，成為兩個世界之間橋樑的象徵，展現出人類即使在戰爭中，也會傾向於尋求共同點。

隨著1945年日本投降而結束戰爭，中國面臨著從總體戰狀態過渡到和解與重建的艱鉅任務。美國以後勤及顧問任務的形式為中國提供軍事援助，協助日本軍隊有序撤離，而透過航拍，美國海軍第七艦隊也記錄了這段過渡時期。戰爭期間普遍物資匱乏的情形為了日後政治格局的重塑奠定了基礎，尤其是中共的崛起，並加速社會和文化的變革，進一步推動戰後中國的非凡現代化。

究其實，戰時中國對於後世的影響交雜著犧牲、韌性與再造。在這個敘事當中，每個普通人的奮鬥最終都促成了巨變，並為中國的現代化進程奠立基礎。

参考資料
References

1. Brett Sheehan, Wen-hsin Yeh, *Living and Working in Wartime China*. Hawai'i : University of Hawai'i Press, 2022.
2. David Stephen Gordon Goodman, "Reinterpreting the Sino–Japanese War: 1939–1940, peasant mobilisation, and the road to the PRC" *Journal of Contemporary China*, 22(79)(2013).
3. Diana Lary, *The Chinese People at War*. Vancouver: University of British Columbia, 2012.
4. John M. Anderies, Marco A. Janssen, Elinor Ostrom, "A Framework to Analyze the Robustness of Social-ecological Systems from an Institutional Perspective" *Ecology and Society*, 9(1): 18.
5. Rana Mitter, "China in World War II, 1937–1945: Experience, Memory, and Legacy." *Modern Asian Studies*, 45:2(2011).
6. Ronan O'Connell, "How China saved more than 20,000 Jews during WW2": https://reurl.cc/YYb4r0.
7. Schoppa, R. Keith, *In a Sea of Bitterness: Refugees During the Sino-Japanese War*. Cambridge: Harvard University Press, 2011.
8. Stephen R. MacKinnon, *Wuhan, 1938: War, Refugees, and the Making of Modern China*. Berkeley: *University of California Press*, 2008.

歷史影像 5

戰火和平：抗戰時期美軍眼中的中國
Peace Beyond the Frontlines:
American Soldiers' View of China During WWII

喆閎人文

創 辦 人 / 楊善堯
學術顧問 / 皮國立、林孝庭、劉士永

主編 Edit / 楊善堯 Yang, Shan-Yao
作者 Author / William Tang（唐銘遠）、Ethan Cheung（張健宣）、Aiden Zhang（章容添）
翻譯 Translation / 楊宗翰 Zong-Han Yang
審閱 Proofreading / 陳榮彬 Rong-bin Chen
設計排版 Design Layout / 吳姿穎 Wu, Tzu-Ying
策畫 Collaboration / CompassPoint Mentorship

出版 Publish / 喆閎人文工作室 ZHEHONG HUMANITIES STUDIO
地址 Address / 242011 新北市新莊區中華路一段 100 號 10 樓
　　　　　　　10F., No. 100, Sec. 1, Zhonghua Rd., Xinzhuang Dist., New Taipei City 242011,
　　　　　　　Taiwan (R.O.C.)
電話 Telephone / +886-2-2277-0675
信箱 Email / zhehong100101@gmail.com
網站 Website / http://zhehong.tw/
臉書 Facebook / https://www.facebook.com/zhehong10010

初版一刷 First Edition Brush / 2025 年 6 月
定價 Pricing / 新臺幣 NT$ 350 元、美元 USD$ 12 元
ISBN / 978-626-99335-6-3 (平裝)
印刷 Print / 秀威資訊科技股份有限公司 Showwe Taiwan

版權所有 · 翻印必究
All rights reserved. Reproduction will not be tolerated.

如有破損、缺頁或裝訂錯誤，請寄回喆閎人文工作室更換
If there are any damages, missing pages or binding errors,
please send them back to ZHEHONG HUMANITIES STUDIO for replacement.

國家圖書館出版品預行編目 (CIP) 資料

戰火和平：抗戰時期美軍眼中的中國 /Ethan Cheung(張健宣), William Tang(唐銘遠), Aiden Zhang(章容添) 作 ; 楊宗翰翻譯 . -- 初版 . -- 新北市 : 喆閎人文工作室 , 2025.06
　　面 ;　　公分 . -- (歷史影像 ; 5)
中英對照
譯　自 : Peace beyond the frontlines : American Soldiers' View of China During WWII
ISBN 978-626-99335-6-3(平裝)

1.CST: 中日戰爭 2.CST: 報導文學

628.5   114007265